About the author, illustra

Richard "Snakehips" Dudanski. Re 1952, Isle of Sheppey, U.K.

Finishing a degree in zoology at Chelsea College in 1974, was invited by his friends to occupy the vacant drum stool of a fledgling rock band rehearsing in the basement of a neighbouring squat...

This musical memoir traces the author's life in the corrugated-iron clad ruins of West London's Squat Land during the two years immediately prior to the Punk Explosion of '76, playing with Joe Strummer's seminal garage band "The 101'ers" in the spit-and-sawdust music bars of the capital. The thrills and spills of a crazy, quirky, hand-to-mouth existence gives way to relative disenchantment with the oncoming of the Punk Uprising, which for the author represents, at least partly, a sell-out to the Machiavellian Managers, as much as the vaunted revolution in British popular culture.

After an aborted venture with the iconoclastic "Tymon Dogg and the Fools", a stint with Lydon's Metal Box period "Public Image Limited", a term with the Dantesque-dub of "Basement Five", Dudanski's tale relates the ups and downs of his involvement in a myriad of bands forming part of a fringe underground London scene through the late 70's and 80's - "Bank of Dresden", "The Raincoats", "The Tesco Bombers", "Vincent Units", "The Decomposers", and his eventual move from London to Granada...

Esperanza Romero (b. 1956, Melilla, Spain). Aged 17 travelled independently from Malaga to London. A multi-faceted artist, studied Ceramics (B.A.) at Camberwell School of Art (1977-81), and obtained an M.A. from the Royal College of Art, London (1982-85). From her own workshops first in London, later in Granada, has created a continually evolving body of work encompasing the disciplines of Ceramics, Painting, Drawing and Engraving. Has exhibited in the galleries and museums of many european countries, the U.S., China, India and Japan. Partner of Richard since 1974 and mother of their two children. Many of the drawings included in this book were sketches made "in situ" 30 - odd years ago.

II

SQUAT CITY ROCKS
protopunk and beyond. a musical memoir from the margins

By Richard Dudanski

Illustrations by Esperanza Romero

Copyright 2013: Dudanski /Romero

Dedicated to:
Esperanza,
M&D, my English & Spanish families
and to: Big John, Dave G, Mole and Joe.

Notes on Images
    All illustrations drawn by Esperanza Romero
    (Except Bramley's poster Ch. 15, & Raincoat's poster Ch. 16).

    All photos by Esperanza Romero , except:
    - Ch. 3: "1st Gig at The Telegragh, Brixton", by Ray Eagle
    - Ch. 3: "Outside That Tea Room", by Ray Eagle
    - Ch. 4: "Joe, Esperanza & Paloma", by Richard Dudanski
    - Ch. 5: "Paloma & Esperanza on boat", by Richard Dudanski
    - Ch. 9: "Joe & Richard, in conversation", by Julian Yewdall
    -Ch.12: "The Raincoats at The Marquee", unknown
    - Ch.12: "Esperanza & Richard", by Simon Bramley
    - Ch.13: "Pil at Manchester", by Dave Crowe
    - Ch.14: "Basement 5", by Dennis Morris

Thanks to the above for use of their images.
Thanks to Ximena Hidalgo for help in cover design.
Special thanks to Richard Davies and Trevor Warren for copy-editing and suggestions…

"..no problem for a besaddled biker with repairs to do on his machine!!"

Table of Contents

Chapter 1 - Squatland 1
Chapter 2 - 101 Walterton Road 16
Chapter 3 - A Spanish Sojourn 24
Chapter 4 - A Rhythm and Blues Orquestra 38
Chapter 5 - Stretching Wings 64
Chapter 6 - Barbed Wire Blues 83
Chapter 7 - Devils in the Chapel 92
Chapter 8 - Snot Rag and a Snarl 102
Chapter 9 - End of the Road 112
Chapter 10 - An Interlude 122
Chapter 11 - Cinderella Transformations ... 126
Chapter 12 - Getting Around 138
Chapter 13 - No Birds do Sing... 148
Chapter 14 - Back to School 158
Chapter 15 - Breakdown and Away 172
Chapter 16 - Rainstorms and Dogg 191
Chapter 17 - Decomposition 203
Chapter 18 - Spain Again 212
Chapter 19 - To the Present 227

Chapter 1   Squatland

A dull thud. Another. A rhythmic thumping, which I at first confuse with my temple's muffled pulse on pillow. Familiar forms become distinct as the early morning twilight filters in through meagre, makeshift curtains. Another sound – an alarmed blackbird screeches up the street. Again a banging from below. Of course. It's them. It's them and their night prowlings. A slow rhythmic thudding from below. Could be many things. Not to worry. Turnover, cuddle up, back to sleep … and … that … dream …

It's morning. The weekend, so no hurry. She's gorgeous and she's next to me, but she is a very slow waker. I bore from plying her with my unreturned attentions. Mattress on the floor, a draped-over suitcase as a bedside table. A threadbare mat covers part of the floorboards. Practically all my possessions picked out of a builder's skip, or from a street market, more often than not left behind by an irate stallholder anxious to get home late on a Saturday afternoon. On a rickety table my records, a clarinet, some books … The daylight streaming in now. How I love this room. Two tall bay windows from floor to ceiling. A large, leafy sycamore outside, and little noise from the street. Ah…that noise last night, was it a dream or … a thudding downstairs…all night a dull thudding.

- "Did you hear it?"
- "Hear what?"
- "The noise they were making. Our friends… I woke to a banging….."
- "Something ..maybe…"

We finally get up and stumble down a flight of broken stairs, no carpets of course and almost without banisters. The bathroom is basic. No bath but at least with a noisy old heater for hot water. The kitchen is stark. Cracked panes in the window looking out over a stretch of barren land. The muffled cries of a couple of kids kicking around a football. The gas stove is filthy. A week old heap of empty booze bottles in a corner, old fag ends rotting in their dregs. Dirty plates and cups piled in the sink, vying for space with a mass of tea leaves and other unidentifiable vegetable matter. No other movement in the house; our fellow occupants, the night Prowlers, are in their daylight land of dreams. Esperanza, my girlfriend, goes round to the corner shop while I put the kettle on. I pour the Shreddies into a couple of chipped bowls. Hang on. There's something wrong here. It's the cutlery. So that was the racket last night. All the spoons and all the forks, as flat as pennies. What a strange imagination! The Prowlers' latest midnight amusement - banging out flat all our culinary utensils. The forks weren't too much of a problem, but have you ever tried eating your cereal with a flat spoon?

Maida Hill, west London, summer 1974. The area mostly dilapidated with rows of corrugated iron–clad houses awaiting an uncertain future. Streets of empty council houses mingling with boarded-up shops, a half empty hospital and the inevitable abandoned cinema, but it had a couple of good Irish pubs, while the sizeable West Indian immigrant population added a spice that the drab and drizzly Harrow Rd couldn't quite douse... My house had known better times, but still retained traces of its former grandeur. Number 86 Chippenham road, between Shirland road and Elgin Avenue. Squatted, but definitely classy. A flight of ten or so broad stone steps leading between a pair of Doric columns to the front door. On entering, your first impressions might begin to waver. A strong smell of petrol. No door to the first room on your left, and the remains of its splintered door frame hanging off the broken plaster. Black oil marks on the floor led the way to a partially destroyed staircase.

The squat had been opened up by the Prowlers some months before I arrived. It wasn't the first time that I'd lived in the neighbourhood. The previous year I had been staying in another squat around the corner in Walterton Rd. It had been in the last year of a degree course I was taking, but for the final three months I had to make a temporary move; study was impossible for me in that house. Far too many distractions. So, with the exams finished, I had come back to the area, looking to reinstall myself. Over a half of

"…as if throwing cats out of first floor windows was normal practice…"

bitter one night in the Chippenham Arms I had met Nick of the Prowlers, and he'd offered me a room in their house. I didn't know him or the mate he was with: a very large, hairy, fat, bearded biker with a blotchy red face, and an incoherent mutter, but Nick seemed ok. Housing problem solved. Back in the neighbourhood and with my friends up the street in number 23, and round the corner in 101 Walterton Rd.

I soon discovered that Nick had other strange acquaintances living with him apart from the Bear. B.S.A.'s and Bonnevilles, benzedrine and booze were their loves. The entrance flight of ten steps was no problem for a befuddled biker with repairs to do on his machine. A couple of planks leading from the pavement to the front door had apparently solved the problem. I never saw their entrance, but the proof was there. Two semi stripped down 750's in the ground floor front room.

The only real problem I ever had with them was over a cat. It was before I'd met Esperanza and I was living alone in my fine, first floor, front room. I didn't know exactly how or from where it came, but occasionally a young cat would trip in through one of the front bay windows from an outside balcony. With a disconcerting assurance it would twine itself around my legs and settle down on a vacant cushion. Flattered by such a display of confidence in me, and happy to share my space with this part-time pet, I looked forward to these sporadic feline visits. One afternoon a friend of Nick came in to my room for something or other. He saw the cat and in one swift move picked it up and threw it out of the open window. I hit the roof as the cat hit the pavement, and all he did was stare at me in amazement, as if throwing cats out of first floor windows was normal practice. I went down to the front of the house expecting to find, if not a mangled corpse, at least traces of the mishap, but there were none. Life in this neighbourhood, for cats and humans, required the full quota of lives.

There were few dull moments in 86 Chippenham Road, although generally the day was more peaceful than the night. It was usually after the pubs had shut that my companions would start to enjoy themselves. One night I spent trying to sleep as they fine - tuned a spluttering carburettor on the Bonneville, and another night of crashing and banging had given rise to the sorry state of the stairs. I had come down one morning with the banisters in a mangled heap in the hallway. But what was amusing was their own subsequent reaction to this their latest antic. When I came back later the same day it was to sheepish grins and "sorry 'bout last night". There they were, hammer and nails in hand, attempting to repair their previous night's excesses.

Most of their escapades were harmless, but occasionally things did get a bit out of hand. I was in my room going about my business. A knock on the door. For some reason I never quite understood, the prowlers maintained a respectful distance from my area in the house. It was Nick:

"Rich. Come up on to the roof. Have a butchers at this."

We climbed out onto the roof and saw, ducked down behind a parapet, the Bear, as usual the front of his tee-shirt soaked with sweat and booze, a couple of other Prowlers, a carton of wine, and a couple of joints on the go. A right regular little party, with everyone in a strange and overly happy mood. There was an expectancy in the air, the reason for which I was soon to discover.

"Get yer 'ead down and look out over there!"

Next to our abode at number 86, there was an empty plot and beyond it a derelict house looking as if it had not been touched since the London Blitz. It wasn't really squatted but I knew that from time to time it was used as a doss-house by tramps. Suddenly, a shadowy figure sneaks out from the front garden, and within seconds a flash of fire erupts from a window. The basement is ablaze in no time at all. My companions on the roof also erupt – in a cackle of mirth, heightened by the arrival of police and fire-brigade.... suppressed giggles like ten year old kids. I confess that for me the arrival of the law is a relief ....what if the winos had been in there sleeping off their sorrows?? I should have been down there to make sure they were safe, instead I'm dumbstruck on the roof like a courtier on Nero's balcony...

*

Survival was never much of a problem, helped of course by the fact that our material needs were kept to a minimum. Temporary part time work was usually available, and as a student I'd inevitably find holiday jobs to supplement the small grant that I received. We often found work through a "cleaning agency" – that would send you up to a posh house usually in St John's Wood or Golders Green, or a smart office in Marylebone. My last assignment, however, had given me a nasty shock. Three days a week to a small house in Hampstead owned by a seventy year old widow. Very cushy I thought, until one afternoon the booze got the better of her and a bird like hand clutched at my crotch as I washed the dishes. Not wanting to hurt the lonely soul but utterly repulsed, I disentangled myself from her amid sobs and sadness. No more cleaning in Hampstead for me.

Nick did me another favour apart from finding me a room. He told me of a job he'd had at the Ascot domestic boiler factory on the North Circular Road in Wembley. Awful conditions but well paid he'd said, just talk to Mr Borrow the personnel manager. I've never liked interviews, and perhaps for that reason felt I had to impress Mr Borrow with something more than I actually had to offer. Anyway, I remembered from my school geography that Clement-Ferrand in France had been a centre for the French steel/metal industry, and started to spin a yarn of how I had been working in a factory in central France using lead plating technology etc...etc.. From the glint in his eye I don't really think that Mr Borrow bought my unnecessary story, but he did give me the job. I later realized that it was probably because no one else in their right mind would have wanted to take it.

First day in and I'm introduced to Terry. He'd been in the workshop where I was destined for five or six years and I wonder if the lead had actually got to him. He was Jamaican, slow moving, kind, and immensely powerful. There are certain special factors about this job which I ought to mention. First, our kit. Overalls, rubber boots, huge rigid rubber pinafore from chin to shins, rubber gauntlets to the elbows, helmet with cloth protector down the back of the neck, and a heavy-duty, scratched, moveable plastic visor on the front. Second, the weather. A rare, hot, very hot, London July. Third, the work shop. Badly lit, badly ventilated, and in the centre of which loomed a huge round vat in which an evil mix of lead and zinc bubbled and fumed. At one end of the shed were various pallets each with thirty or so burnished copper Ascot inners – serpentines they call the twisting tubes. At the other end a stack of empty pallets, casting a sardonic glance at the two grotesquely robed creatures, at least one of whom while stumbling in the semi-darkness wondered if he hadn't regressed to the time of Blake's satanic mills.

For about four weeks I accompanied Terry in the ritual. A perverted baptism of fire, as we clamped the serpentine on to the heavy iron jig, one of us at each end, facing each other. As if in training for an Olympic weightlifting competition we "snatched" the jig to chest height, dipped it in an acid flux and then ever so slowly lowered our baby into the angrily spitting molten lead …..spin off the excess… plonk it on to the mocking empty pallet…and back for the next one, and the next… and the next…. It was with a mixed reaction that one day I arrived at work to find pickets at the factory gate. All-out strike to complain of abuse of health and safety regs. Marched down the north circular with Terry and the union banners, and never went back there. I had been earning good money though, and for what it was worth had built up my biceps.

One inconvenience of squat dwelling and such a job had been the lack of a decent bathroom. After a sweaty day's toil, a shower was a must and that necessitated a visit to an institution much appreciated by us squatters: the public baths. Dating from a previous age, we used the baths in the Harrow road next to the canal, and some others up in Kilburn Park. Huge wrought iron tubs with scalding water that rushed from ancient brass taps with a fury that I'd never seen before or since… Only the pervading whiff of disinfectant clouded the experience. Also available was the cheapest clothes washing facility in town and the most efficient clothes drier ever invented: massive steel racks on rollers that made use of hot air produced in the boiler rooms. The other users of the installations seemed as old as the place itself. The "washer-women" always seemed to have bundles of clothes on the go - they must have been taking in other people's laundry to make a few bob on the side, but they were very friendly towards these new young-uns, and had plenty of advice to offer us:

"That's right dearie ….. fold it down the crease … an' don't forge' to shake i' out tonight when you get 'ome…. Give us an 'and wiv this 'ere sheet before you gaw, will ya luv…."

*

So who were these squatters? Can we talk of a genuine organized squatters movement, or was the house where I lived in Chippenham Road typical – which I suppose you could say wasn't too far removed from a psychiatric ward. Did a squatting community really exist? It is difficult to generalize as there was such a variety of people involved, and an estimated squatter population in London of between twenty and thirty thousand in 1975. There were, for sure, many people in serious situations with a desperate need for housing, and then there were people more like ourselves, who apart from the saving on rent, found in it the means of creating a living space on their own terms. The ideals of freedom behind the young person culture that grew throughout the 1960's, saw the beginnings of a squatting movement where the motive of Liberty blended with what previously and in less affluent times had been a dire necessity of the poor and the homeless. The idea of occupying vacant property or land has no doubt existed from when our forefathers roamed the plains looking for shelter in caves. Closer in time we have that event in English history when Winstanley's Diggers unsuccessfully squatted common land in St George's Hill, Surrey during the post revolutionary fervour of the mid 17th century, confronting the more pragmatic politics of Cromwell's cronies. This and other similar actions particularly from the 16th to the 19th century were often the only recourse available to the poor in response to the widespread "enclosure" of land perpetrated by landlords.

Walterton Road, Maida Hill, 1974

Then we have the salutary reminder of state hypocrisy demonstrated by the Government's reaction to the chronic housing problem that arose in 1945/46, with the arrival of thousands of men and women during demobilization following the 2nd world war. This state of affairs gave rise to the "Vigilante" movement of squatters, resulting in the occupation firstly of disused military camps and then of uninhabited properties throughout Britain, culminating in the famous squatting of one Kensington block by 1500 people.

Of course, the housing problem and the squatting movement in late 20th century Britain pales in significance when we put it into a worldwide context. The United Nations Survey on World Housing published in 1974 gives an idea of the huge scale of the phenomenon:

- *Current statistics show that squatter settlements already constitute a large proportion of the urban populations in developing countries. In Africa squatter settlements constitute 90% of Addis Adaba, 61% of Accra,*

35% of Nairobi.... In Asia 29% of Seoul, 67% of Calcutta .... In Latin America 60% of Bogotá, 46% of Mexico City.......

The situation as seen in the third world was and is overwhelmingly a result of rural to urban population migration. In 1970's Britain, and I think in most "developed" countries, the situation was very different and the composition and the motives of this Squatting Community were extremely varied.

The houses that we took over came from various sources. The great majority belonged to the GLC, London's municipal corporation. There were hundreds of houses, often a whole street, left empty for years awaiting re-development. Another landowner of note, especially in our area of west London, was the Church commission. Goodness knows how the gentlemen members of the commission rationalized their flagrant disregard for their Founder's commandments, but there they were sitting on the deeds of millions of pounds worth of prime west London real estate, and most of the time quite happy to remain sitting on it while house prices rocketed hand in hand with the numbers of London's homeless.

As I've mentioned the houses could be in an awful state of repair, so anyone who did decide to squat would usually have to put up with, putting it lightly, a pretty basic standard of living. Often the GLC would send in workers to trash the installations so that they couldn't be squatted. Obviously this could be more or less of a problem for us, depending on the assiduity of the council labourers. We quickly learned the basics of plumbing and even the electrics became less of an unknown. However, few squats in our Maida Hill neighbourhood had a bath, some were without a cooker, no carpets, no washing machine and dodgy wiring. Security of tenure just didn't enter into the equation.

Among squatters, young people were the great majority and immigrants were another important element. To the weird Biker Boys of my house in Chippenham Road, other rooms were soon occupied by friends of friends ...in that case a Colombian, Argentinean and Peruvian. Around the corner in Elgin Avenue there was another house with Brazilians in the majority, and there were a number of Chileans, some recently escaped from Pinochet's coup. Irish, Spanish, French, Australian, the list of nationalities is endless. Any young person landing in London, whether from the sticks or from abroad, who was not too worried about the normal comforts of life, could solve the serious problem of finding affordable rented accommodation. Added to this was the possibility of living with friends in a manner not possible in a normal rented flat.

As a result it was usual for each house to acquire a distinct identity. Some were very organized, veritable communes, whilst others were disaster areas – inevitably the junkie or wino houses. Likewise the political attitudes of people involved were varied. Some had a strong political motivation (Socialist Workers Party et al) but they were a pretty small minority. Some were pure idealists and perhaps saw themselves as direct descendants of Winstanly's non-conformists, and others as pure blooded Anarchists. Squatters of course had no single defined political line, although from a practical necessity many self help groups appeared. The Advisory Service for Squatters (ASS) was foremost amongst them, and then most of the London boroughs had their official squatters group – Kilburn, Tower Hamlets, Maida Hill, Clapham....

In Maida Hill, the main political push came from a house in Elgin Avenue where astrophysicist Piers Corbyn was the main mover. He was a man with incredible energy and ability to motivate others. He was always available to give advice, and apart from galvanizing a united effort he also edited the local squatting magazine EASY. The problems of Elgin Avenue led eventually in late '75 to a stand-off with the GLC and police, but Piers masterminded a successful victory from behind the barricades with all the squatters being re-housed.

The offices of "Release" were also in Elgin Av – an emergency legal service very useful when having to deal with what were relatively frequent brushes with the law. The simple act of squatting was I think a political statement in itself. Although we often had good relations with our direct non squatting neighbours, the majority of people saw us as a bunch of scroungers jumping the housing queue, and public opinion was certainly influenced by the national and local press, almost all of which, but especially the "gutter press", were strongly against us. The Sunday People mounted a specific campaign against the phenomenon with headlines such as *"SQUATTERS' ARMY – shock truth about the won't pay rent brigade"*, suggesting the existence of armed squatter hordes preparing to overturn honest capitalist society.

It was to be later, in early '75, when bleary eyed I answered a knock at the door of 101 Walterton Rd. Despite his greasy gabardine he seemed an ordinary enough sort of bloke as he introduced himself as a reporter from The News of the World. More the fool me! We had by that time formed a rock group and I thought a bit of press cover might do us good, so was happy to invite him upstairs. To start with it was really quite amusing. Every question he had was angled at the sexual mores of the Squatters: groupies, drug use, you name it... Then he started ogling at my girlfriend – we were both still in bed after a late night - as I think he probably started hoping he might even get in on some of the action he was so busily imagining! What a schmuck. We quickly got fed up with it, and he got very upset when we told him to get lost, and we ended up literally having to throw him out.

A week later there appeared his article in the paper tattling on about the orgies and drug taking in a West London squat. I believe the article was the first to coin the phrase "Squat Rock" when referring to our group – a description I was particularly fond of. Looking back, and especially when you think of the manner in which just twelve months later Malcolm Maclaren successfully manipulated the press to the Sex Pistol's advantage, I can't help but think now that just maybe we had missed an opportunity. Could our Squat Rock have given the tabloids the scandalous headlines that were to appear a year later with Punk? We'll never know, but all the juicy elements were there! However, through a mixture of naivety and a keen disrespect for the "established", there was no way we wanted dealings with the whited sepulchres of Fleet Street. You should have seen the lecherous, pin-prick eyes of that hack!!

Our other main adversary at the time was the Metropolitan Police Special Patrol Group. They had been formed as some kind of inner city Civil Guard. They were to be met frequently in our neighbourhood, especially at night, and especially if you were young or/and black. Their activity was normally "stop and search", and they were usually heavy handed and insulting. When you think that they spent all night, half a dozen blokes cooped up in a transit van with nothing much to do on their agenda, it's hardly surprising that when they did stomp out of their van, they were looking for trouble.

One memorable day of confrontation occurred in January of '74. It had occurred to the GLC that one way of getting rid of the squatter menace was to refuse the London Electricity Board (LEB) permission to supply electricity. Early one winter's morning we had a very heated discussion with LEB workers who had been sent down to dig up the street outside the house and cut off the supply. With the arrival on the scene of babies in mothers' arms from houses further up the road, we finally managed to persuade them to go home, but things were coming to a head and joint action was organized. About seventy of us met up in Kensington Gardens, and after a quick meeting with Piers at the head, we decided to march on the LEB offices in nearby Notting Hill. A delegation of half a dozen or so entered the building and barricaded themselves in; refusing to leave until a boss came from head office to talk to us. Meanwhile the rest of us hung about outside, handing out pamphlets explaining what was going on. All was pretty good humoured until a hero cop tried to get in through a window on the 1st floor. Someone shut the window on his fingers, although from his screams you might have thought we'd cut his arm off. Within minutes the Special Patrol Group, who had been lurking round a corner, came at us with truncheons flailing. Battered and bruised we did at least manage to solve the problem, with the GLC eventually backing down from a court case that was not looking good for them. The Electricity Board were obliged to supply us, on the same terms as any other applicant.

There were a number of self-help groups in our area, apart from the Maida Hill Squatters Group and the Release offices in Elgin Avenue. A useful contact was "The Rough, Tough, Cream Puff Estate Agency" down in Westbourne Park Road (send sae), rumoured to have been founded in 1281 by a certain Wat Tyler. A friendly, good humoured organization, it was indispensable when looking for a new squat to take over.

That Tea Room

Their updated lists of empty properties read like the brochure of your poshest Kensington estate agents. It was edited by local neighbourhood squatting luminary Heathcote Williams, and connected to Tony Allen's "Rough Theatre", pioneers of the soon to flourish "alternative" comedy scene.

For us, however, the most important institution in the neighbourhood was most definitely "That Tea Room" near to the canal at the top of the Great Western Road. It was everything that a good café should be. Long tables knocked together from sleepers left by the side of the Great West railway, it was the inevitable meeting place for a cuppa with friends. Whether a Mozart concerto or a Buka White blues, good music would always be playing, and the food would be a relief from the normal egg, bacon, chips, and beans served at the greasy-spoon cafes in the area. Most memorable for me though was the atmosphere inspired by the people that ran it: Dave and Gail, from a Jewish background in Manchester, and their friend Jeannie who had been living with us in 101. Kindness personified the three of them but always with a twinkle in the eye, they had time for everyone and anybody, which often included the most down and out of the down and outs....

Chapter 2   101 Walterton Road

My first contact with the Maida Hill area had been through my brother Pat. He had just been evicted from a squat in Penryn St, Somers Town, and with his friend Simon Cassell, came to the area in early '73 via Simon's friend Gail, who lived with Dave at 23 Chippenham Rd. For anyone who had contact with it in those days, the house holds special memories. This squat was the antithesis of the biker house that I was to live in, in the same street, a year later. For starters, Dave was a very handy man, so all the normal comforts were on hand – a bath, carpets, wonderfully functioning kitchen etc.. But more important, there was that same open heartedness which was to later characterize That Tea Room. Living in the house were Dave and Gail, Liz, Tymon Dogg – with his baby grand piano inexplicably crammed into his shoe box bedroom at the top of the house, Doctor Dave available for any medical emergency, and Gillian the painter. There was a continual stream of visitors apart from the regular inhabitants. You would walk into the living room and never know who to expect to see, head poking out of a sleeping bag on the floor. The social life of the neighbourhood revolved around the house, especially throughout '73-'74, and it was through Dave and Gail that Pat and Simon were told of a house around the corner at 101 Walterton Road.

Walterton Road runs north off the Harrow Rd and Elgin Av. Treeless, lined on either side by four story Victorian terraced houses, the number thirty one bus would trundle down it, on its way from Camden to Chelsea. Owned by the GLC, one side of the street had been converted and the other side, our side to be, was awaiting rehab. Some houses had been demolished, others had been trashed almost beyond repair and the rest were sitting idly behind corrugated iron defences. As we have seen, these defences were not difficult to breach and a large number of houses were soon occupied. Number 101 was at the north end, not far from a pawn shop and the Chippenham Arms in Shirland Rd. Entry was easy, and in Spring '73 Pat and Simon were joined by Simon's girlfriend Pam, and Nigel (Gail's brother) and Jeannie. On visits to my brother Pat, I soon realized that this was the place where I wanted to live. I was offered a room on the second floor, gave notice in my bed sit, and moved in round about September '73. Other friends were also quick to enter the house. Jules, from Pat and my home town of Leek in the Staffordshire Moorlands. Antonio, a Chilean friend of Simon. John, a travelling Australian, who was instrumental in the introduction of a very important member of the household – Trouble (alias Charlie, alias Charlie Pig Dog), an abandoned mutt with an injured leg....

The house was little more than a bare structure. The bathroom had been destroyed, and the electrics mostly ripped out. Dave supplied piping and know-how to set up a gas cooker in the kitchen, and a rudimentary "re-wiring" job was put in hand. Connecting up to the "company head" in the basement was as hair raising as you can imagine, as Woody would later describe it – "Plugging in direct to Battersea Power station", and our basic installation would entail stringing a cable from the fuse box to each floor. Inevitably the fuse would be replaced by a chunk of silver paper from a cigarette packet to withstand the excessive load, and sure enough one winter night a mass of wires caught fire due to the overload from our electric heaters. The bathroom was too much to repair. Apart from using the public baths up in Kilburn Park, we eventually picked up a second hand tin bath – little bigger than a washing tub, and an old water heater, which we kept in a basement room along with the bicycles. This sometimes resulted in an untimely visit whilst bathing, but that didn't worry us much. What was annoying was that the only toilet in the house was outside in the yard at the back of the house. The kitchen was rudimentary and small. I don't remember much cooking being attempted, but the old gas cooker served well in keeping us warm as we sat around the flaming burners, sharing a spliff and drinking tea from jam jars.

We made do with the absolute minimum, and I think were very content with our lot. Sometimes we would wander down Portobello Rd market at the end of the day, and pick up for free enough fruit and veg for the week from what had been left behind.

The kitchen 101 Walterton Rd

    Portobello and Golborne Rd were in fact pretty essential to our existence! Second hand clothes, shoes, furniture, books, records … you name it and you could find it down the market for next to nothing.

    Thumbing through boxes of old vinyls was my special delight. It might take you eight stalls before you found something, but finally there it was, a gem, and your heart would start to race as you fumbled the disc out of its cover to check for scratches. Very occasionally you might come across the collection of someone with a similar taste to your own, and that was like hitting a gold mine!

There was the other side to it though. Inevitably with that kind of music-buying you would sometimes end up with rubbish, having been seduced by a beguiling cover...... or intrigued by the liner notes. Whatever, the good ones are there today on my shelves, still with their 50p price tag, and with memories intermingled in their grooves...

Living on a shoe string didn't permit an extravagant social life. The old Electric Cinema Club in Portobello was cheap and invariably there was something interesting to watch. The late night sessions were favourite, with two films for the price of one. These were days before the prohibition of smoking in cinemas, and at the Electric this benevolence extended to the consumption of stronger smokeable substances, despite the inevitable tell tale aroma. Our drug consumption was pretty much restricted to hash and grass. The acid craze had more or less been and gone, speed and coke we hardly saw, and smack and downers were just not wanted, at least among us. There were several good watering holes in the area, and there was a bonus in that many pubs put on a group for free. We had the Windsor Castle little more than a stone's throw away on the Harrow Road. Then there was the Cock up in Kilburn, the Western Counties in Praed Street .. One night we came upon Dr Feelgood with Wilko Johnson playing the Windsor Castle, and there were other good bands playing around – Kilburn and the High Roads with Ian Dury, a local group called Phoenix, Alberto y los Trios Paranoias ...

We didn't differ from the great majority of our peers in that music was so important to us. It was, and is, as if in our godless society it had taken the place of religion. Its very essence, amorphous and mysterious, reaching to those places of our psyche which maybe before were catered for by religious belief. It seems to me as if the pop concert hall has taken the place of church as a place for mass worship. From the adulation lavished on pop stars, I'd say that there is further proof!

I had never learned a musical instrument, but my Dad had always been a great music lover and from an earliest age allowed us to play his 78's on the gramophone. Beethoven's violin concerto was my first love, and I remember conducting a concert or two with my Mum's knitting needles. On acquiring a stereo, our appreciation of different music extended hand in hand with the expansion of Dad's record collection – Bartok, de Falla, Stravinsky, or Debussy crashing out at full volume. As we got older we were encouraged to buy our own records when we had spare cash, and my elder sister hit the Beatles mania – "She loves you", "Please, please me" , The Searchers, Gerry and the Pacemakers, etc.. as they were charting in the early 60's.

Down the market...

It's funny. As an eleven year old, I was to take the Beatles very much for granted. A lyric such as "Love, love me do" was enough to put them into the "soppy" category. Later with "A hard day's night" etc, they were to partially redeem themselves in our eyes, but never completely. I had a passionate craze with The Shadows buying all their singles, before rapidly moving to the early Who, the Small Faces, Spencer Davis, The Animals etc in the mid sixties. At 15 years old in 1967, black American soul became my favourite, without doubt linked to the convergence of dance music and girls at the local hop. The Temptations, Isley Brothers, Otis, Wilson Picket, the Barkays, Arethra, Sam and Dave, accompanied Prince Buster, Max Romeo and co, of mid sixties rude boy ska.

Inspired by a gig caught in a local pub, the first LP I bought was Geno Washington and the Ram Jam Band "Live". I later had it confiscated at school for being "jungle" music!!! By the late 60's Hendrix, Cream, Pretty Things and then all the psychedelic stuff arrived, but they didn't quite knock Soul of the top of my list, and I also got interested in Jazz – "Take five" being the stimulus to buy a Duke Ellington compilation and other vinyl that caught my eye in second hand shops. Of course, apart from the Beatles, the Stones were ever present, and my brother Pat complemented my tastes with a love for Dylan and a strong hankering for the Blues.

With hindsight early seventies popular music did perhaps lack the thrill that the sixties had had, but at the time it didn't seem like that. For me music wasn't restricted either to the charts or to the rock sections in your record shop racks, and the specialized rock press just didn't interest me. Half the things I bought were classical discs and jazz. There were bands that stuck out though. Captain Beefheart was tops. A gig he did at the Rainbow in I think '72 was unforgettable, with the Magic Band of the "Clear Spot" era. His big attraction was, of course, that he was genuinely different, a true original. Trout Mask Replica wasn't an album that you'd play every day, but when you did, you knew it was something special: like a Bartok quartet or an obscure Albert Ayler disc. Other things that come to mind are Dr John, Soft Machine, Van Morrison, Frank Zappa, Alex Harvey, and still good soul with the likes of Curtis Mayfield, and how can I forget Lol Coxhill's "Ear of Beholder" LP ....It doesn't stop! Once you start making mental lists of music you love, you feel you could never end...For every band you mention, there are three more that come to mind. Glam wasn't my favourite, but Bowie as Ziggy, unpretentious Slade, Roxy Music and Bolan had their moments, and for me were at least preferable to the symphonic mega bands that were the flavour of the day.

*

The early seventies found me down in London studying a Zoology degree course at Chelsea College. I say studying, but truth is there wasn't much of that. There wasn't that much Zoology for that matter. I was able to choose courses that interested me, and ended up spending most of my time in the humanities department where some great young lecturers led small group tutorials in Psychology, Sociology, Literature and Philosophy of Science. In my last year I ended up writing a paper on just about the most obscure subject I could find – the views of the so-called 19th century Nature Philosophers who represented an alternative view to the classic positivist science of their time. My choice of subject was just a further reflection of my "looking for something else", and rejection of the normal path that would lead to a respectable career in perhaps some Glaxo research and development laboratory investigating the soporific effects of dinitrobenzoamanine on the nervous system of a lesser speckled Ethiopian gerbil. These were days of a frenzied idealism, where "if it felt right – do it" was the maxim. I didn't know exactly what I wanted to do, but I knew what I didn't.

So, returning to 101 in '73, it shouldn't surprise if I were to say that music was, if not yet an obsession, half way to becoming one. Pam was an accomplished flute player, Nigel had a baritone sax, Pat started with the guitar, as did Simon who also, inspired by Nigel, bought a beaten up alto from a pawn broker in King's Cross. I'd always loved the sound of a clarinet, so when I saw one going cheap down the market I forked out the readies. I was very undisciplined about it. I didn't have any lessons and didn't read music, but I worked out a few tunes by ear, "Strangers on the Shore" being the first, and then a song called "Wild Man Blues" taken from a fantastic Johnny Dodds disc recorded in the late 20's that I had picked up.

There were, however, other artistic interests in the house apart from music. John the Oz devised an ingenious method for raising a few bob. He placed an ad in "Time Out" suggesting a rendezvous at a certain time at the ticket office of Marble Arch tube station. For a small fee he offered the possibility for the public to witness original, improvised "Tube Theatre". I went down with him one evening and there met with half a dozen or so inquisitive customers. We paid our pound and were instructed by John simply to observe him, and to remain as anonymous as possible. It all came quite naturally to our antipodean actor as he was continually on the edge of insanity anyway. He very subtly intruded into the fragile civility of London Transport's passengers. A slight twitch in his upper lip would gradually develop into a grotesque grin, and then to uncontrollable limb jerks, accompanied by a manic chattering:

- "Madam, do you really believe that the Queen has the divine right to feast on hot sausage dogs for breakfast, whilst two thousand three hundred and sixty four bats, residents of the northern section of this very red line of the underground system of the capital of the realm, are in dire danger of under nourishment due to the excess ozone, result of ....etc ... etc..."

I really can't imagine what the unaware audience of this theatre thought, as John's mad world was laid bare. At the climax of John's "Existential Alienation Show" there would be a burst of applause from the "in the know" spectators, and we would bundle out of the carriage to wait for the next train, and John's next unsuspecting victims!

Life in the squat was full of like escapades. It was fun and it was crazy, but there reached a point in March '74 when I realized I just had to get out if I was to finish my degree. I had three months before the final exams and decided to live a hermit's existence for that time in the quiet flat of a quiet friend. I moved to Holland Park, studied, did the exams, and came back as quickly as possible to Maida Hill in June '74; which brings me to where I started this tale. On returning, there was no room at 101; Alvaro a Chilean friend of Antonio, had moved in during my absence, which precipitated my meeting at the Chip with Nick that I have already mentioned at the beinning of this tale, and my acceptance into the Prowlers' house, around the corner at 86 Chippenham Rd.

Chapter 3   A Spanish Sojourn

Back in Maida Hill. My exams finished and the start of summer. I remember it being a euphoric time. 101 had expanded with new occupants. Alvaro, a Chilean musician friend of Antonio. Woody, a friend of Tymon and Gillian, recently moved up from Wales, and Roz, had all moved in. With our friends around the corner in Chippenham Rd, and other houses in the neighbourhood, we were a large closely knit group of people.

Antonio and I would knock about together, and he was friendly with other South Americans who were later to move into my squat at nº 86. Something very special for me occurred one hot July evening. We both liked jazz, and used to frequent various pubs that featured live bands. One of these was the Hoop on Notting Hill. Among the crowd we spotted a couple of girls up at the front, and Antonio, never slow where females were concerned, was there in a flash. He discovered they were from Malaga, and arranged to meet one of them – unfortunately the one I'd also fancied, at a later date. A week or so later, again in a live music pub, this time down in Gloucester Rd, there she was, but apparently not too involved with Antonio. I made a move and by the end of the night was very keen indeed on finding out more about this 17 year old Andalusian gem, who, being called by the name of Esperanza, at least gave me reason for optimism, her name meaning Hope in Spanish.

Well, I kept at it and kept at it, not being much encouraged by the fact that she had a steady bloke back home in Spain. She was an au pair for a horrible Chinese couple in Shepherds Bush that gave her little more than white rice and a very hard time. Oh God, what I wanted to give her! Finally, under the stars in a queue for tea at Windsor Free Festival I stole a first kiss. We had to return a day early from the festival, and so missed the bloody police charges to break up the event (after all, we had been squatting the Queen's back-garden!). I remember travelling back with her through Notting

Hill on the top deck of a bus. It must have been August bank holiday weekend, because the carnival was in full swing beneath us, this of course before the event became the enormous street festival of later years. I persuaded Esperanza to move in to the squat with me, but time was running out for us – she had her return ticket booked for a flight in a couple of weeks time, and I had plans to visit friends in Barcelona.

The reason for coming back early to London from the Windsor festival was a certain event that we had pencilled in for the 14th of September, but this needs some explaining. I have talked about the obsession with music that gripped the original occupants of 101. Simon was learning the alto sax and Pat had got hold of a bass. This was furthered by the arrival of Antonio who had experience with the drums, and then of Woody, who at a previous stage had learned chords from Tymon Dogg on various busking expeditions and had later gained some experience in a band or two down in South Wales before coming to London. Earlier that summer, Antonio had managed to borrow a drum kit from a squat up the road which he installed in the basement of 101. Similarly, the other equipment was assembled from various sources until finally there was enough gear for a group rehearsal. As Simon Cassell was later to comment:

- "I can remember the first band session in the basement of 101, with Pat, Woody, Antonio and me ...... I can't remember what we played, some rock'n'roll tune, but it had real energy and I remember afterwards we all thought, yeah we've got a band here."

Over the next few weeks the rehearsal room was "conditioned" as much to deaden the sound as to stop the sound from leaking outside. This entailed stuffing a mattress in front of the window and nailing a carpet or two to the walls. Broomsticks as mike stands and beaten up old amps with their valves open to the air were the order of the day. By the end of August, Alvaro who was a tenor sax and piano player and who had in fact had success with a pop-rock band back in Chile had also started playing with the fledgling group, and apart from adding an element of musical experience to the proceedings, it was he who came up trumps with the offer of a possible gig at a Chilean Solidarity Campaign concert in South

London. There was a problem though. Antonio had just left the country on a visit to friends in Germany. The band was without a drummer.

Rehearsal Room 101

Meanwhile, my musical endeavours with the clarinet had been supplemented by the acquisition of an old pair of bongos, which in turn had led me to the occasional solitary bash-around on the drums once they had been installed in 101. With little to lose by trying, I accepted the suggestion to sit in on a rehearsal, I suppose you could say an audition. With no small element of surprise I was subsequently offered the drum stool, which can only lead you to imagine the rudimentary nature of our music. Shock horror when suddenly we were informed the gig had been brought forward a week! I had less than a week remaining to get my act together!

It was just as well that the music we played was basic to an extreme. For the gig we prepared six songs, all of them R&B standards: "Bony Maronie" – Larry Williams, "No particular Place to Go" and "Roll Over Beethoven" – Chuck Berry, "Gloria" – Them, and "Hoy, Hoy, Hoy", a lesser known song by Chicago blues man Little Johnny Jones. The sixth song I'm not certain of, but think probably it was Eddie Cochran's "Summertime Blues" or maybe Berry's "Around and Around"….. the mists of time are thick at times. I got hold of a pad, and for quick reference wrote the structure for each song in my own notation. Something like:

  - *Intro count Woody, pause, BANG, BANG, BANG, Side/side 1ST verse, Solo Alvaro, verse 2 &3. END change Up/down, 4 times riff, Kerplunk for dead END".*

Woody was my drumming mentor those days. Apart from having owned a kit before lending it out to a friend, he was a Chuck Berry/ Bo Diddley fanatic, and their music was to be the source for my crash course in drumming. We had a very basic system for classifying the rhythmic feel, the songs being either "Up and Down" or "Side to Side": the former being a straight rock beat, the latter with more of a syncopated shuffle feel. This was hard and fast rock and roll with a BIG FAT snare-drum back beat interspersed usually with one or two thuds on the bass drum in each bar. It was pretty obvious that what was essential was not to lose the beat, and usually the song ended faster than it had started. This of course was much more preferable than to it slowing down. For someone coming in to drum with no experience, this music was perfect. There was no finesse required, just energy and application, and I loved it.

1st Gig, The Telegraph, Brixton. Woody & Pat

Alvaro (billed for the gig as "El Huaso" – a Chilean term for Gaucho) took the solos on Tenor, Big John sung most of the songs (and took out his alto on some) while Pat, Woody and I concentrated on the rhythm, Woody also taking the mike on a couple of tunes. "El Huaso and the 101 All Stars" made their debut at the Telegraph pub in Brixton the following weekend. The poster I have says Friday, 6th September. I am pretty sure it was a Saturday - it had that Saturday afternoon pub feeling. Whatever, we turned up at the gig to support the reggae band "Matumbi", although we had an uncomfortable wait as they arrived late having had problems with their van. El Huaso was appropriately dressed in poncho and wide brimmed sombrero. The rest of us kitted out in our normal attire – myself with a hat that was a fixture I virtually slept in, Woody with a very old leather jacket barely held together at the seams …. "Image" was not a concern. When Matumbi did arrive we had to ask them if we could borrow their amps and drums for our set. No problem. Real cool bunch of geezers as they sat smiling through our set and barely had time to come on and do their own.

So we had done it! Our friends, naturally enough, were enthusiastic. A number had come down south of the river to hear us and the general feeling was – "when's the next one?" For me though, things were complicated. I had only been with the group a week, drafted in as a stand in, and with other plans in mind. Increasingly attracted to things Hispanic, I had booked a flight to Barcelona with a vague arrangement to meet with friends of Antonio. Within a week of the gig I was on a plane to new climes and unknown adventures. A week after I had left, Esperanza was to head home to Malaga and her novio, and meanwhile the band awaited the return of Antonio before its next outing.

*

My first contact with things Spanish had occurred as a child and in curious, dreamlike circumstances. Until the arrival of adolescent black-heads and the excruciating dilemma between the desires of the flesh and the demands of the Church's moral, I had been a firm believer in my ancestral Roman Catholic faith. This resulted in my being a willing altar boy, which for the uninitiated, translates as being one of those angelic faces robed in ankle length red cassocks and white pinafores, who would assist the priest during mass. I knew the Latin responses by heart, would handle the wine and water cruets, and would breathe in deep the pungent smell of incense that wafted from the dangling crucible.

I had a weekly assignment that necessitated my waking at six in the morning to accompany Father Golding to a local Spanish "enclosed" convent. You might think that for any young lad this would be a most horrendous duty imposed from above. Not so for me for two reasons. Firstly, and most importantly, after mass the priest and I would be led to an ancient glass conservatory overlooking the convent garden where we were served the most incredible breakfast I have ever encountered, before or since, both in terms of quantity and variety. Where the Spanish nuns had acquired this wonderful skill in English breakfast I didn't bother to question at the time, as the smiling sister trundled out endless supplies of delicious food.

The other attraction was the mass itself. The nuns, who were of a denomination that shunned all contact with the outside world, would be ensconced, completely out of sight, in a choir loft at the back of their chapel. It was just as well that they remained uncontaminated from beyond their convent walls. Their presence was felt by the most beautiful music that they made during the sung mass. It was like nothing I had ever heard. My Dad's love of Manuel de Falla's orchestral music had introduced me to the haunting tones of Spanish music, and I was accustomed to the Gregorian Chant - inspired music of the high mass, but this was something else. It would send a chill over me as their strange and mysterious voices uplifted to the heavens, and I would strain my neck to try and catch just one glimpse of the beings that created such sounds…

The nuns, however, were of a very different ilk to the Spaniards that I encountered on the very hot, muggy September night that I arrived in Barcelona. As I wandered down the Ramblas, like many people before and after me, it was love at first sight. Its unfamiliar smells; its language I didn't recognize; a city seething with people at four in the morning; the bars down the Barrio Chino overflowing with sailors and hookers; the rats scuttling among the rubbish heaps, and a hundred and one other details that were new to me. It was too late for me to look up my friends and I was happy to roam the streets until the early hours. As a teenager I had hitch-hiked round Italy and France, had stayed in a commune squat for a few days in Amsterdam, been picked up by the cops in Germany…. but had been nowhere with a flavour such as this.

I eventually found a park bench, put my bag beneath it and laid out flat with my hat over my face. Consciousness arrives with the dawn and the sound not of the happy twittering of Catalan bird-life, but rather that of my back-pack (clarinet included) being ever-so-slowly dragged over gravel from under the bench. What to do? I can't see the thief without moving. From beneath the brim of my hat I can just spy a spindly hand on the end of my bag strap. A quick decision is needed, and I decide to launch a surprise attack. With the quickest movement I could muster, my arms flailing the air and screaming at the top of my voice "What the fuck!!!" no dagger gets planted in my chest, and the poor tramp scuttled away, hopefully with the fear of God in him.

My welcome to Spain was rectified later that day when I met up with Lola and Carmen, two contacts Antonio had given me. Both would become become firm friends, and they helped me settle in quickly. I found a room in a house with Pepe, and started getting around the city. What a place! The Barrio Gotico, the Gaudi architecture, the Picasso museum and the national museum with its Romanesque figures, Tibidabo … and to top it all a vibrant sea port. Ports have always fascinated me. They have that ephemeral air, a feeling of never ending horizons, of transience and possibilities, which I find both reassuring and exciting at the same time. The port in Barcelona was right there in the centre of the city, with its flag-topped towering hulls here today gone tomorrow, rusty chains, and spider-like cranes … Maybe too it's the sound of the fog horns. I was born, and as a child had lived on an island – the Isle of Sheppey situated in the Thames estuary where it opens out into the North Sea. As I lay cuddled up in bed trying to keep out the cold, I would sometimes hear the conversations of the ships horns as they made their way to the London docks, crawling blind up the estuary in thick fog. A large ship with a long and deep booming call, answered by a smaller, no-nonsense shallow drone, maybe a tug or pilot's boat coming to meet it. And then what must be a monster liner, it must be huge, as it angrily delivers its urgent warning wail.

Back in Barcelona, what was most electrifying for me was the atmosphere in the city. This was still Franco's Spain, but at a point when people, especially young people, and very much so in Catalonia, could see the changes coming around the corner. In contrast to the stale state of affairs in English culture, here was a feeling of expectancy, of hope in a future, of an imminent change to something better, to freedom... I mixed with a diverse and colourful group of people, mostly artists and musicians, who knew that after almost 40 years, things couldn't remain the same for much longer. And then there were the more mundane but very important details of everyday life. The wonderful fresh coffee for breakfast, cigarettes that cost literally next to nothing, the easy possibilities of teaching English part time to survive, the fantastic food and cheap restaurants, good cheap wine, and most important - the beautiful girls.... But talking of girls I had Esperanza very much on my mind, and an invitation to visit her down south in Andalusia. After a couple of weeks I decided to make the trip, and went via a boat to pre-rave Ibiza, and then after a few days on another one to Alicante. I arrived in Malaga, had a great time, but ... what can I say? I am not one for sharing my loved one with someone else! The triangle broke on a scorching, dusty, drunken Granada afternoon, and I caught the train back to Barcelona thinking that was the end of that.

Back in Barsa I sorted myself out with work, played a lot of clarinet, and all but forgot about both drums and Esperanza. Most nights I'd meet up with friends in a café down by the port, and then head off to the bars and clubs. I remember concerts by Tete Montilu in the "Zeleste" night club which was a firm favourite of ours; Miles Davis at the Jazz Festival in the incredible Palau de la Musica, and innumerable small gigs forming part of a lively music scene.

I decided to go back to Blighty for a week at Christmas to see family and friends, naturally leaving most of my gear and the debt of a month's wages owing me from the language school where I had been working. But before relating the subsequent events, I must record, albeit not being from my own first hand experience, what had been happening to my friends in 101 since that first gig down in Brixton.

*

Antonio had returned from Germany in late-September and the group had got back to rehearsing. The severe shortage of equipment was partially relieved when Woody, with the help of Simon, went down to Wales to recuperate his gear, which included a pair of Linear Concorde amps (without cases) and a guitar or two. To this Woody was soon to add a VOX AC30, one of the classic guitar amps of the period. The L.C. amps needed seeing to and Woody found the neat solution in a couple of draws from an old chest. The custom cabinets finished, the band had a rudimentary PA.

Rehearsals continued, but gigs weren't easy to find. The name now changed to "THE 101 ALL STARS". One gig, with I think something to do with the fellow west London band Hawkwind, was in an abandoned cinema in Lancaster Rd off the Portobello: the infamous Meat Roxy. Behind a rudimentary stage, a banner was daubed with the following slogan.

- *CIVILIZATION HATH TURNED HER BACK ON THEE.*
  REJOICE, SHE HATH AN UGLY FACE.

Pat remembers the place being more akin to a swimming pool than a concert hall. A large double bed in the middle of the auditorium rose like a North Sea oil rig from the sheet of water that covered the floor. Electricity came from a squatted house to the rear of the building and almost certainly didn't come with earth protection. Didn't someone say that water and electricity is not a happy combination? The band played through their set, gingerly picking those guitar strings. The next gig was a short affair. Once again the Chilean connection helped, with the offer to play at an "Arts Festival for Chilean Resistance" at the Royal College of Art. You can imagine the shock-horror of the organizers as the 101'ers blitzed into their first song. As Woody commented:

- *"We started playing Bony Maronie, and they went 'Get this Capitalist Rock'n'Roll out of here!'"*

One can only imagine that they had presumed El Huaso was to be accompanied by charangos and Andean pipes!

The 101ers play the Charlie Pig Dog Club

At just the right moment, Liz , a friend living in 23 Chippenham Rd, had the spark of an idea and suggested starting up our own club. She went down to the Chippenham Arms just fifty yards from 101, on Shirland Rd, and spoke to the landlord. Downstairs it was pretty much your normal spit and sawdust boozer, faded red flock wallpapered walls, and half a dozen regulars slouched over their Guinness. But upstairs there was a large unused "functions" room, just waiting to be put into operation. Lizzie charmed it off the publican for just a pound a night and the band suddenly had its own club a stone's throw from the squat. The first "event" was held on 4th December, and the venue was baptized after our hound "The Charlie Pigdog Club". Very often the dog would contribute more than just his name. Whether from complaint or a desire to participate, inevitably he would wail in unison with the saxes as they were tuning up, and sometimes even in the middle of a solo!

This was the ideal situation for a group to start getting itself together, and virtually every Thursday for the next four months the Chippenham Arms would reverberate to the sounds of the 101'ers. Especially at the start, it was very much a club for friends and the local squatters. There are reports that Alvaro actually prepared sandwiches (to sell?), but what is certain is that entry was 10 pence per person, and even this would cease to be charged once the band had been bought a drink, paid the rent, and maybe a little extra kept for broken strings. Before and after the performance a mike would be thrust in front of the speaker of Woody's Dansette record player, the musical offering being similar to that which the band was in to playing – a sultry Howlin' Wolf blues or maybe a Chuck Berry rocker.

The basic line-up was the same as it had been for the first gig down in Brixton, except for the brothers – Richard and Patrick. I was off in Spain and Antonio of course had taken back the drum stool on returning from abroad. Pat had decided he'd had enough, explaining to Woody over a pint in the local Skiddaw pub, he left with the enigmatic:

- "I can't believe we're in a group... So I'm going to leave..."

Simon then asked Mole to come in. Up to that moment a guitarist, it wasn't too much of a change for him to take on the bass. In fact it suited him down to the ground. The Mole, living in the depths of Notting Hill just off All Saint's Road was a reggae freak. All Saints was very much the centre of Jamaican Notting Hill Gate. From amongst the wreathes of ganja smoke that perpetually hung over the pavements outside the Mangrove club, you would feel as much as hear the bass-heavy throb of a latest Joe Gibbs or Scratch Perry cut. Mole took to his new instrument fast. Apart from the bass amp and cabinet he brought with him to the band room, he would also bring in a Bob Marley song or two, although the only reggae that was ever performed in public was the Desmond Dekker standard "The Israelites".

Outside That Tea Room. From left: Paloma, Clive, Mole, Jules, Woody, Trouble (aka Charlie Pig Dog) Alvaro, , Esperanza, Dave G, Richard.

Additions to this nucleus would vary from week to week. You couldn't describe it as a jam session, and it was certainly more than a rehearsal, but friends would sit in on different songs – Barbie on harmonica, Clive on lead guitar, Jules on vocals, Tymon on violin,

Sean on more harps... So this was more or less the situation when I came back to London for a week's break at Christmas 1974. This and also the presence of Esperanza who had decided she'd had enough of life in Malaga, and had decided to return to the squats of West London.

Chapter 4   A Rhythm and Blues Orchestra

Within a few days of my arrival, Antonio once again decided to leave for foreign climes, and once again I was asked to deputize on drums. This was now a "serious decision time". My clothes, a pay check, a job, a girlfriend and a way of life I loved were waiting for me back in Barcelona, but here in a cold and wet Maida Hill squat there was something very special happening; this and the fact that the girl I really wanted was also here. I didn't need to think twice. I never saw again the clothes I'd left behind, and I am still owed a month's wages by a language school in Barcelona...

Esperanza's taste of London Squatland the previous summer had been enough for her to recommend it to her sister Paloma when she had returned to Malaga the previous September. Within a couple of weeks Paloma had come over with her Bolivian boyfriend Herman, and they too had been offered a spare room in 101. Add to this the imminent arrival in the house of another Spaniard – photographer Rocco from Pamplona, and the Swiss girlfriend of Jules, and you can imagine the tower of Babel that 101 had become.

The first gig, second time round so to speak, that I was to do with the 101'ers was of course in the Charlie Pigdog club. Once again I was in at the deep end. Their set had grown from the six songs we had knocked together for the Telegraph gig, to more than double that, and with a degree of steadiness (if not to go as far as to say sophistication) that I was hard put to keep up with. I had little choice but to practice like a maniac, fortunate at having Woody and Mole accompanying me in the rhythm section, both of whom were willing to spend hours and hours going through things with me, apart from the rehearsals with the rest of the band, and my solitary practise time. My hands were a mass of burst blisters from the sticks, and I adopted a dubious trick I had once been told by a Paddy on a building site: "whenever you have to relieve your bladder piss on your hands, and be jeezus see how they'll toughen up!" Very hygienic, I would think, gingerly steadying a loaf with the tips of my fingers whilst preparing a marmite sandwich.

By mid January Clive had been invited to join the band on lead guitar. An old acquaintance of Woody, he had been in the audience for the first gig back in September, and had since sat in on various occasions at the Pigdog. He was what we would have called a "proper" musician. He'd been playing for years, new all the licks, and for that reason was a great help to the band, both at live gigs and during rehearsals with his ability for arranging songs. The line-up was now Jules on most lead vocals (and maracas), Simon on alto sax, Alvaro on tenor, Clive on lead guitar, and Woody, Mole and myself in the rhythm section. In fact lead vocals would also be taken by Simon, Woody and later the odd song by Mole. Add to this the appearance of guest musicians on various songs and you had a veritable Rhythm 'n' Blues Orchestra, which is how we styled ourselves.

The horn section was an important part of the sound, and of course a number of the songs in the set reflected it. "Good Morning Judge" by Wynonie Harris, "Choo Choo Ch'Boogie" by Louis Jordan, and "Hoy, Hoy, Hoy" by Little Johnny Jones were all versions of late 1940's Blues Shouter-style early rock and roll. The saxes also featured of course on other songs such as Van Morrison's "Domino" and "Gloria", and Alvaro being an accomplished player and arranger, worked out sax parts for the rest of the set. Chuck Berry was represented by "Roll Over Beethoven", "Maybelline", "No Particular Place to Go" and more. We did an extended versions of both Howlin' Wolf's "Smokestack Lightening" and Slim Harpo's "Shake Your Hips". Other fifty's R'n'R tunes were "Slippin' & Slidin' by Little Richard, "The Hand Jive" by Johnny Otis, the Coaster's "Smokey Joe's Café" sung by The Mole, and of course some Bo Diddley standards. A couple of early Jagger/Richards and Lennon/ McCartney tunes were I think our only nod to the 60's apart from the Morrison songs and the Velvet's "Sweet Jane" , and so you might be excused for thinking of us as a R'n'R revivalist band. But we weren't, at least not in a conscious sense. It was more a question of using the simplicity of structure that basic R'n'B offered us, as a vehicle for an extremely high octane fuelled rock that hurtled along at a speed and intensity that would leave most quiffed Teds aghast at our sacrilegious versions. We were definitely not (and technically incapable of being) a Crazy Cavan type genuine R'n'R band. Other R'n'B based bands playing the pubs such as Ducks Delux, the Kilburns, or Chilli Willi and the Red Hots were incomparably more accomplished than us, but for playing hard and fast we had the edge. I think probably the Dr. Feelgood Band of the time was the only live group that in any way we identified with.

The first song of our own that I remember doing was an Alvaro number called "Rubber Hammer", and this recollection is almost exclusively restricted to the vision of El Huaso hammering out the chords on the old piano we had in the band room in 101. But yes, we did finally get it into a Pigdog set on a couple of occasions. The Pigdog Club certainly was going from strength to strength. What started as a homely affair mostly for our friends, soon developed into a regular haunt for anyone looking for some rock and roll action, and each week the crowd would grow. We would still trundle the drum kit and amps down the road from the squat in an old pram, and we would still set up the Dansette for some light entertainment between sets, although sometimes Tony Allen's "Rough Theatre" with Tom Costello would put on a "Silly Old Bastard's Liberation Front" show.

Alvaro's sandwiches were replaced by a packet of cheese and onion crisps, and a pickled egg if you fancied it, from the bar downstairs, but woe betide you if you left a handbag unattended upstairs in the club. We started having trouble with thieving, a tea leaf or two dropping the bags out through the windows to their mates waiting below. Towards the end of our tenure we also had the odd fight, and I think eventually the Old Bill put pressure on the landlord to get rid of us. A couple of times the police would turn up for no particular reason, and the Special Patrol Group would be parked round the corner during gig nights. After all, during this period there was an on going confrontation between the GLC backed by the police, and the organised Maida Hill squatter group. Basically the police would take any opportunity to harass the local squatter community, and this was just one of them.

Police arrive at The Charlie Pig Dog Club...

Later that year Allan Jones, another old friend of Woody, was to write a piece in Melody Maker, setting out his impressions of the club:

- " It was some time back in February that I first saw the 101'ers. They had a residency in the Charlie Pigdog Club in West London. It was the kind of place which held extraordinary promises of violence. You walked in, took one look around, and wished you were the hell out of there. The general feeling was that something was going to happen, and whatever that something was, it was inevitably going to involve you. After ten minutes glancing into secluded corners half expecting to see someone having their face decorated with a razor, the paranoia count was soaring.

The gig that particular evening ended in a near massacre.

As the 101'ers screamed their way through a 20-minute interpretation of "Gloria" which sounded like the perfect soundtrack for the last apocalyptic days of the Third Reich, opposing factions of (I believe) Irish and gypsies attempted to carve each other out. Bottles were smashed over defenceless heads, blades flashed, and howling dogs tore at one another's throats, splattering the walls with blood... No one, I was convinced, is going to crawl out of this one alive....."

Allan must have been in a particularly sensitive mood that night. I don't remember there ever being razors and blood be-splattered walls; maybe I was too busy bashing the skins, but by the end of our stint in the Chippenham, the club had achieved a certain notoriety, and at least punters would be guaranteed an exciting Thursday night's entertainment.

Meanwhile we were taking the music very seriously indeed. Having a weekly gig was perfect for getting the band off the ground and we practised day and night. As any fledgling rock band knows, finding gigs is always a problem, and it was just as well that we had the Pigdog Club. Live gigs are essential to a young group. I can't imagine a group stuck for months in a rehearsal room without the feedback of an audience, for me a group's music feeds off it being heard.

I had an unpleasant decision to make in mid February when my friend Antonio came back from his trip to Germany and left me hanging uncomfortably on the horns of a dilemma. The group had worked hard during the six weeks of his absence. For me the band had fast become the be all and end all of existence. A majority of the band wanted me to stay on as drummer, and so…. c'est le vie. I was confirmed as resident of the drum stool. Mea culpa, Antonio. We had a scare one day when the owners of the kit appeared, wanting their property back. Woody and I pretended to be Spanish, not knowing anything about a drum-kit. It gave us a breathing space, and I managed to cobble together a kit from a dealer down Portobello who specialized in very cheap drum gear. It was to serve me well for the next six months by which time I had saved enough to buy a new Pearl kit and some decent cymbals.

Our relations with the neighbours were varied. At one point Simon had his sax stolen. Pat and Woody did the leg work around the neighbourhood, and eventually found it being played by a Brazilian in Elgin Avenue. He had bought it in good faith from the thief who lived a couple of doors up from us in Walterton Road. The geezer had even been round to commiserate with Simon over the theft!! Anyway the Brazilian good naturedly gave the sax back to Si, and I wonder if he ever got his money back from the bloke who had nicked it. There was also of course cooperation amongst the houses as well. The squat next door which was the base for another band – "Phoenix" had their electricity linked up to our house, and friends in another house up the road had lent us the drum kit.

The band room was now at the back of the house in the basement. I have mentioned the rudimentary "sound proofing" that we had installed, but it wasn't to the satisfaction of all our neighbours. I remember one night a shouting match with someone living nearby that ended with Simon being threatened with having his "fucking legs cut off" which did have its comical side as Si towered over everyone at 6 foot 5!! Not so humorous was the response of some neighbours who lived in a squat in Chippenham Rd that backed on to a stretch of wasteland which also backed on to our yard. Midway through a rehearsal someone went to use the outside toilet and came under gun fire. It was only an air rifle, but Jeannie got hit in the face, and panes of glass started getting broken in the kitchen window. You actually felt as if you were pinned down by sniper fire until I think it was Tymon, Pat and Si who rushed round to the house and put a stop to it.

Big John

It was a neighbour, Charlie, the bass player from Kilburn and The High Roads, who managed to get us a support spot with his band. We had been hard at it for nearly two months now with daily rehearsals and the weekly Pigdog Club, and were itching to spread our wings so to speak. During this time we had only had one outing down to a private party in Brixton, where if I remember right, Twink and the Pink Fairies also played. The gig with Ian Dury's band at Chelsea College, seemed like a big step forward. Apart from being support to one of the few groups around that we appreciated, it was our first gig on a proper stage with monitors and a decent PA! This also resulted in recruiting a sound man to handle the house sound. Mickey Foote was a friend of Gillian and Woody, and was living in Chippenham Rd at the time. During the Pigdog gigs he would lend a hand and gradually we came to rely on him in the string-changing sound-mixing department. Apart from being a good mate, he had a good pair of piano-man ears, and was unflappable: all essential characteristics for a PA mixer-man.

Another first time appearance was in the transport department. Up until now, the old pram had served well enough to wheel our gear from 101 to the Chip, but a couple of days prior to the Chelsea gig Simon had come up trumps with a very special vehicle. He had found an early 1950's Austin A50 Taxi converted to a hearse, big enough to take all the gear and half the band. The occupants of 101 chipped in a tenner each, and we ended up with a battered, though stylish and practical motor for a hundred quid.

The club lasted till the end of April, but meanwhile changes were occurring in the composition of the group. Even if you have never played in a band, it is easy to imagine how difficult it must be for a balanced relationship between members to endure. I'm amazed that any group keeps going, and when you have strong creative personalities (which of course is what is necessary if you want a good group) the greater the likelihood of serious ruptures. Very often what happens in a rock group is that commercial reasons become the only incentive for a band to continue, the members hating each other's guts but sticking it out as long as the pay cheques keep coming, which of course was not the situation that we were in. Tensions were inevitable though; sometimes simmering under the surface; other times exploding in a row, but generally we had a great time. All of us except Clive and Mole (who lived down the road) were living in 101, and maybe also it was the thrill of a new experience (for the majority of us it was our first group) that kept us in such good spirits. The band had started naturally as a venture between friends and initially there wasn't a sole leader. Serious decisions were taken in a democratic way – sensible discussions then a vote, but as the band developed and evolved it was only natural that a leader should emerge. To an extent this process was, I think, as much a case of default as of positive planning.

Alvaro was the first to go. I really can't remember clearly the circumstances, but I am pretty sure that it was his idea, or if not, then he certainly wasn't too unhappy about it - whoever had made the decision. It is only a guess at motives, but I think probably his interest started to wane from when his close friend Antonio hadn't been accepted back in to the band. I had the feeling also that he didn't really think that much of our efforts. After all, he had had more than ten years at it, and some of us not ten weeks! Whatever.... he'd given us his experience right at the start when we had virtually none, and he'd got us the first couple of gigs. He was a genuine off the wall character and a great laugh to be with. Check out Squeaky Shoes Records.

The next to go was Jules. In fact he didn't leave completely, because having agreed with the rest of us that fronting the band wasn't really his thing, he became our hustler for a time, finding us gigs and generally lending a hand. But where he really did contribute was with his camera. Devoting himself to photography, most of the best shots of the band came through his lens which he was later to publish in 1992.

So, now we were down to five – Mole, Woody and I in the rhythm section, with Si on alto sax and Clive on lead guitar. It seemed to be a logical progression. With fewer members the rehearsals were more controlled. Communication was easier and it seemed as if we could work more efficiently at the music. Woody was by now a much stronger figure in the band. He had a gigantic obsession with what we were doing, and his progression as a potent frontman was meteoric. The Pigdog residency helped us all to develop some basic skills, and by the time Jules left the band, Woody had developed an economic style on guitar concentrating on the basic rhythm, allowing him to take on most of the lead vocals. To describe him as a passionate performer is an understatement. His rhythm guitar style might have been simple, but what was lacking in skill was more than compensated for by a force and aggression that left his heavy gauge bottom strings dancing in the wind night after night... Likewise with his singing, a coarse, gruff howl delivered with a virulence that left any onlooker with no doubt as to its veracity. Not only that, but he was a creative force in all senses.

He started writing songs for the band, usually the words and melody. The first song was "Keys to Your Heart", and it was just as well Mole reacted the way he did when Woody hummed and strummed through his first composition. Woody would later comment:

- "I played it to him and he went 'Oh, that's bloody good that is'. That gave me the confidence to try and write another one. If Mole had said 'That stinks', I would have packed it in right there!"

Usually Woody would come up with the lyrics and an idea for melody and chords, and then develop it further with Clive, before bringing it to the band room where we would all knock it around until it took final shape. "Keys" was soon followed by "Motor Boys Motor" and "Steamguage 99". Musically, they were very much in the mould of the tracks that we were covering: two and a half minutes of helter-skelter R'n'B. To begin with the lyrics didn't vary much in subject from women and fast living, but within that context Woody was developing his own style, dropping in quirky images drawn from personal experience.

Talking of which, quirky images in a visual sense would also flow from his pen, Woody being happy to knock up an idea for a poster or leaflet. Yet another facet of his inventiveness was in the name department. If you didn't have a nick name when you arrived in the band he would soon make sure you received one. Simon for his height became Big John. Clive had his name reversed to the Evil C (Evil for short) with a fair dose of irony as he was by far the more mild-mannered amongst us. For myself, and I don't know to this day why or from where, I received Snakehips Dudanski, Snakes for short. Mole had arrived as The Mole, and that leaves us with Woody. He too was Woody on arrival at 101, but after a week of Johnny Caramelo, he finally decided on the much more evocative and apt Joe Strummer.

Mole, Joe & Richard

There were other people in the house who also received a second christening. I have mentioned that Esperanza's sister Paloma had also come to live in 101 with her then Bolivian boyfriend. As Woody had said in the first song he wrote for the band:
- *I changed the lock on your heart*
  In broad daylight, you call that a crime?

and Paloma, later to become Palmolive, teamed up with Woody, now Joe. The Piranha Sisters as the two Spanish lasses were to be known, were amongst our keenest fans, not surprising really with one going out with the singer and the other with the drummer. Not, however, in a hanging around back-stage sort of way (not that, to start with at least, we did many gigs with a stage never mind with a back-stage!) but rather as ever present ravers on the dance floor. They were irrepressible.

We had fun one day when we decided to go and give their mother a royal reception on arrival at Heathrow airport to pay her two wayward daughters a visit. At least six of us piled into the hearse (plus of course Charlie the Pigdog), not forgetting to bring along a battered but comfy old armchair for our special guest. This proud, fur-clad, Spanish mother of nine didn't bat an eyelid as the troupe of scruffs led her to our ancient limousine. Did she realize that her chair (which we grabbed by the legs to stop it sliding during the journey) was positioned exactly over the spot where numerous corpses had lain whilst making their last journey? You wouldn't have thought so as she returned the smiles of onlookers with a wave fit for a queen. And what was she thinking as she entered through the decrepit hallway of 101? She must have thought she was dreaming as we led her up the battered stairs, dodging the dangling electricity cables and holes in the floorboards, to take a cup of tea from what was I hope our best china – surely not a jam jar, or just maybe she thought that this was the normal way of living in the barbaric north of Europe. Whatever, she accepted with grace the way of life chosen by her errant offspring, and would happily lay a spread on the grimy kitchen table on returning from a trip to Harrods' food hall.

Apart from special occasions, such as Doña Concha's visit, the cupboard in 101 was pretty poorly stocked. From time to time someone would decide to cook up a dish of something, but usually the kitchen would produce little more than baked beans on toast and innumerable pots of tea. The fact that there were up to fourteen of us living under the same roof didn't help matters, and of course washing the dishes would always be a matter of dispute. As I have already mentioned, we would tend to eat at That Tea Room or at a local cafe, and of course a Jamaican patie or interminable bags of chips were always available from the local chippy.

All of us shared a most precarious economy, but part-time and temporary jobs were usually pretty easy to find, so long as they didn't disrupt rehearsals. I needed to buy a decent drum kit and was lucky in landing a job just fifteen minutes walk away with flexible hours, reasonable pay and the odd bonus in the form of a fine wedge of best quality Stilton, or a miniature bottle or two of whisky.

The Portobello Hotel was not your normal hotel. Recently opened, it tried very hard to be a funky, off-beat establishment, and succeeded in appealing to rich Americans in particular, especially when a record company was paying what would be a hefty bill. Antonio told me about it, and it suited me fine. I would do a night shift two or three times a week, which required my presence in the restaurant/bar from midnight till seven in the morning. I would usually catch the tail end of dinner, but then, being the trendy place that it was, guests would often come back to the place in the early hours of the morning. I would be there to sort out their gastronomic caprices, which usually took the form of nothing more extraordinary than a rare-done steak and salad, or a gin and tonic. The platform-booted, gay receptionist just luuuved hanging out with all these famous people, and was more than happy to cater for the more exotic whims of some of the clients. It was a decadent world of coke, bubbly and money, miles away from our squat existence, but my most vivid memory is of a rather peculiar couple who had come to stay.

They were still finishing off their dinner when I came on for the night session. Very much out of sync with the place they rather looked as if they could have been your very own granny and granddad, up from Bognor Regis. A diminutive, bald headed gent sitting in the corner with his even more unobtrusive partner, winged horn-rimmed specs and crimplene suit, they looked as if they'd just come back from the bingo parlour. Quietly spoken, very polite and pleasant, I took an instant liking to them:

"Excuse me dear, but would you be ever so kind and let me have another glass of that port your friend has served us?"

Yes, it was their ruby wedding and their wonderful son had treated them to a couple of nights up town:

"What a lovely hotel it is, you have all been so kind to us. We've had a very special time haven't we Doris?"

"Yes, Harry, we have indeed. Such friendly people you all are, er … yes I'll just have another tiny drop of that Brandy, the one over there, with the funny label ….."

Nothing like our normal customers, their quaintness was a breath of fresh air and I happily left off the drinks from their bill. Next time I came in to work and I was met by a detective sergeant wanting to ask me a few questions. It was the fifth hotel they had done in a fortnight. All expensive hotels in central London. No one suspected the unassuming old couple as they left the following morning, light of luggage of course and with hundreds of pounds of unpaid bills, and there was I the previous night thinking I had done them a favour by "inviting" them to a couple of drinks!

*

Towards the end of April, the curtain finally came down at the Pigdog Club. We weren't expecting it, and suddenly with no other dates in the pipeline, our regular gig disappeared. I can't remember the details, but I think it was through another "squat rock" band – The Derelicts, based not far away in Latimer Road, that we heard of gigs being put on at The Elgin pub on the corner of Lancaster Rd and Ladbroke Grove, barely fifteen minutes walk from 101.

Squat bop…

The first mention that we were to receive in the rock press had just been published by Allan Jones in the Melody Maker. Not the extended article that he was to write in July, but just a tiny snippet in a piece that I think was about "Bands to watch out for..", or something to that effect. Jules, who had recently swapped from singer to manager, went down to see the publican with a cutting of the article. He persuaded the owner to give us a trial in two weeks time. We played what amounted to an audition, and I remember some complimentary remarks from the boss afterwards (no doubt also influenced by the amount of liquid consumed by the sizeable crowd that came to see us), and thus started a residency that was to last even longer than had the Pigdog Club.

It was a fine pub, more vibrant than the Chip. We were paid a few quid to play a couple of sets in the largish room on the ground floor, straight through from the bars. Once again we had been able to find the perfect set-up to maintain the momentum of the group. Every Thursday we'd be ripping through our songs, and over the next few weeks the crowd grew bit by bit until by the summer it would be packed out week after week. However, having just established ourselves in our new quarters, things were brewing in the band room which were to result in yet another change in the line-up.

From the beginning, Big John had been a big part of the band. Two years before with Pat, he had opened up the house in the first place, and practically a year previously he, Woody, Pat and Antonio had organized the first rehearsal in 101's basement. Getting hold of an alto sax to learn had led him to the real roots of Rock and Roll – the late 40's early 50's black R'n'B, where saxophones were an essential part of the line up. He was also a great fan of Van the Man Morrison, whose music at the time also invariably incorporated a wind section. With Alvaro on tenor and Si on alto, the self-styled Rhythm and Blues Orchestra of the Pigdog era was a fair enough description of aims, but with the increasing influence of Evil's lead guitar on the band's sound , followed by the departure of Alvaro and his tenor, things began to change. More than a little friction between the sax and guitar players resulted.

In the early days, Si would take on a sizeable share of the lead vocals. However, by the time Jules had gone, Woody's confidence and abilities in that department had led to him becoming the lead singer on most songs. The more we played and the more experience we accumulated, it seemed as if a band could function better with one front-man, not two. I don't think there was anything particularly Machiavellian in all this, Woody simply had things very clearly in focus by now. Looking back, there appears to be no reason why Si shouldn't have carried on. He was a natural performer, a forceful personality with a very strong presence on stage, combative, and with a great sense of humour. But it was not to be. The sax as a solo instrument up there on its own with only a year's practising is a very hard act to pull off, especially when those same solos could be taken by an accomplished musician on guitar with over ten year's experience. One day, probably after yet another row in rehearsals, Big John simply announced he'd had enough. I missed his presence a lot. Apart from being a close friend, for me he had always been an essential part of the band especially with his dynamic stage presence interacting with Woody...

So now we were down to four. In the space of weeks, the Rhythm and Blues Orchestra had transformed into a Beat Combo. But things seemed right, and no impetus was lost. The group was gelling more and more as a unit. We were now just a rhythm section, lead guitar and Woody's potent front man persona, with backing vocals from the three of us where necessary. It wasn't a problem for Clive to take over the solos and some of the riffs that had been Big John's. Some of the classic sax songs were dropped, but others such as "Hoy, hoy, hoy" remained long in the set. Meanwhile new songs were being introduced continuously. I remember some ferocious versions of The Kinks' "You really got me", and we added other 60's standards such as The Small Faces "Sha la la la lee" and the early Beatles' "I'm Down", but Chuck Berry remained the principal source of inspiration. Could I ever forget our versions of "Rock and Roll Music", myself trying to squeeze in just the hint of a rudimentary latin flavour for the couple of bars "...down Mexico way...". Other Berry numbers included "Oh Carol", "Route 66", "Too Much Monkey Business", "Johnny B. Goode" apart from ones I have previously mentioned. Other songs of the Elgin period were "Rave on" and "Peggy Sue" by Buddy Holly, and there were also a couple of Elvis songs: "Heartbreak Hotel" and a version of "Money Honey" that was to stand out for a special collaboration.

Although never a permanent part of the band, Tymon Dogg had been a collaborator from the beginning. He was living in 23 Chippenham Road back in the spring of '73 when Pat and Si had first been pointed in the direction of 101. There in the attic, along with his piano, were shaums (Chinese trumpets), a violin, viola, glockenspiel, harmonium, mandolin, guitar, all of which in 1975 he was in the process of using on his first independently produced solo album – Outlaw 1.

The acquisition of his piano had occurred in bizarre circumstances. On the lookout for a decent set of ivories, one day in '73 Tymon spied his quarry through the bay window of a house down the posh end of Elgin Avenue in Maida Vale. It had something to do with the Sutherland Brothers (and Quiver?), and sure enough Tymon received permission from someone in the house to take away the unwanted instrument. A couple of nights later Tymon had assembled a motley crew to lend a hand, and walked down the avenue to collect his booty. There being no one in the house at the time they managed to get in somehow and were in the process of carrying the piano down the front door steps when the unknowing owner appeared on the scene. Not surprisingly, a rumpus ensued, but finally his permission was given. What I find most difficult to comprehend is how they subsequently pushed the thing the mile trek up to Chippenham Rd, and then manhandled it up four flights of narrow stairs without it suffering any permanent damage!

Tymon had been singing his songs, accompanying himself on piano or guitar, since his adolescent days in Liverpool, having toured as support for the Moody Blues in the late sixties and been on the thresh-hold of a deal with Apple, before arguments with his management over "who controls what" set him off on his own very personal road. Around 1972 he acquired a violin which was to gradually replace the guitar as his preferred instrument for live shows, and for this he developed an original position for supporting the instrument (balanced on his arm rather than under his chin) which allowed him to sing or spit into his harmonica at the same time as bow the violin.

Add to this on some songs the use of a harmonium, which he would pump with his left leg to deliver a drone. His performances were unforgettable. Soaring through the whole gamut of emotions, the songs would range from a delicate ballad to a frenzied fling, all based around incisive lyrics and wonderful melodies.

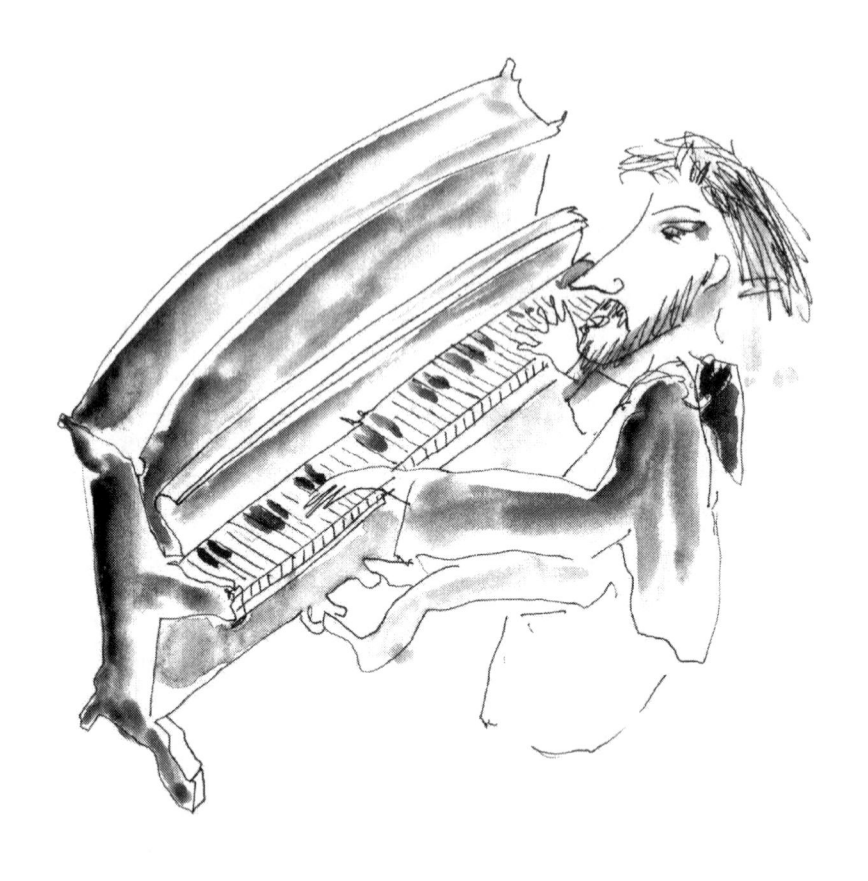

Tymon Dogg

    We now rehearsed a few songs with him, one of which was the afore mentioned Money Honey, the others being his own compositions: "Sick as a Dog" and "Suffer our Way to the Stars" amongst them, which we would feature half way through the set at the Elgin.

    Another rather strange variation in the set was a swop in positions that I would make with Woody. While he took up the drum sticks, I got out my clarinet and we would do a version of an old 40's Duke Ellington favourite of mine – "Tulip or Turnip":

> *Tulip or turnip, rosebud or rhubarb, filet or plain beef stew,*
> *Tell me tell me tell me, dream-face,*
> *what am I to you?"*

I can't imagine how the clarinet solo sounded, and I can't pretend that my vocal cords were ever more than very average sounding, but the idea was to have a laugh, and it was a good excuse to stretch my legs... The song didn't last long in the set, and it certainly never made it onto the set-lists for the various gigs that finally we started to unearth.

One of the main sources for these was our association with various squatter groups in London. We wouldn't get paid for playing the Benefits, or "Squat Bops" as they were affectionately termed (maybe free drinks at the bar), but apart from the satisfaction of a strong feeling of solidarity, it obviously helped in reaching out to a wider audience. One of these gigs, held in Tolmers Square to support local residents' fight against the "Stock Conversion" investment company, was memorable for the appearance on the bill of the legendary Arthur Brown.

Jules was doing a lot of hassling around for us, and his efforts paid off with the booking of various dates, one at our local "Windsor Castle" being among them, but it was through one of our fellow inmates of 101, that we landed what was to be one of the most uninspiring places that we ever played. Rocco was a part-time waiter in a club down in Soho called the Saint Moritz. The name should have given us a warning. That and the fact that Rocco would actually have to don genuine Lederhosen to go to work, but I suppose due to the fact that the club was situated 80 yards down the road from The Marquee and next door to a myriad of seedy strip clubs, we were expecting a slightly more funky establishment than that which greeted us. Mr Sweetie was the owner of this very strange club, whose only clientele it seemed were a handful of very straight-laced Swiss ex-pats. The dozen or so couples in the basement ran to the corners of the room as we yanked up the volume and hurtled through our music. This was a new experience for us as much as for them. It was the first time we had ever been received with such complete and utter indifference and I remember now the odd feeling as we ended the first set to a smattering of applause and the immediate return of the public to the dance floor coinciding with the return of the sweet strains of Abba.

There was some recompense. At least we were getting paid for the job, and secondly Woody, who by now more and more was converting to Joe, extracted a good song out of the experience:
> "Mr Sweetie of the St Moritz,
> We're the ones who play the hits .."

Strangely, Mr Sweetie wanted to repeat the experiment three weeks later. Maybe he'd taken a shine to someone in the band, maybe we were a tax loss for him, maybe he hated his customers, or just maybe the Swiss students had a strange way of showing their appreciation. There was a short debate as to whether we wanted to repeat the experience, but we weren't ones to snub the offer of a gig, especially when a few quid were involved. This in fact became almost an unwritten rule of the group: "never say no to a proposal to play." This was demonstrated the day after a St Moritz gig, when we had the chance of playing at The Stonehenge Festival. Clive in fact was out of action with the flu but we decided to do it as a three piece all the same. We received the somewhat dubious honour of accompanying the rising of the summer solstice sun. In fact I don't remember any sun peeping from behind the banks of Wiltshire mist and drizzle, and precious few people either at six in the morning. Maybe they were all down at our most famous megalithic monument, clawing at the banks of barbed wire erected to protect it from the Druidic hordes. It was their loss. We performed a particularly dynamic set, before heading home for our regular gig at the Elgin.

Dynamics was for me now the catch word when defining our music. Nothing had changed over the previous six months in that most of the songs were performed at a blistering pace. But to increase the levels of intensity, and thus the effectiveness of the music, we had to concentrate on a delicate control and balance in the power applied and the resulting decibel levels within the songs. This for me is a simple but fundamental necessity for good Rock. I can't stand a relentless wall of sound. Basically, it quickly becomes boring. Excitement comes from contrasts, and if we could work to a crescendo even better. Joe was well aware of this fundamental fact of R'n'R, and what a pleasure it was to drop the noise level on the drums down to a murmur behind his whispered wail, the music suspended as if it were in some temporary timeless space, before crashing back in at full volume. It was no coincidence for me that our most successful live songs used this tactic. "Keys to your Heart" and "Steamguage 99" both had middle sections where we'd bring volume levels down to a minimum before cranking the power back up again, and "Gloria" was the example par excellence of this ploy.

I loved performing Gloria which was to remain as our Tour de Force blockbuster final song from the beginning of the group till the end. A classic three chord wonder, it of course depended on keen control of the dynamics. From the first gigs we treated it to extended versions that allowed for a fluid interplay in the middle section. No two versions were the same, and there was an element of improvisation that didn't really exist in the other songs. Joe would launch off into an almost subconscious conversational world of images and ideas, and I loved to lay in off-beat rim shots and shuffles following the nuances of the vocal, all at a manic tempo. The cue back in was three times "who's that knocking on my door?" and from then on in till the end it was a remorseless race to a cacophonous finale which would only end when we couldn't reach any greater intensity of feeling. For me the set would invariably finish with an un-studied demolition of cymbal or snare drum stands, whatever was in the way, as I'd stumble off to the dressing room.

These were very physical performances, especially for Joe and myself. He would be breaking strings at an alarming rate at most gigs, and I would go through I don't know how many sticks, and maybe a snare drum skin or a bass drum pedal with disturbing frequency. This was very uncool music. We would of course finish the gig dripping sweat and myself often with a blood splattered kit, usually from battered knuckles. Many people thought we were into speed or coke or something, but it's a fact that we never touched the stuff. A joint after the gig and a pint or two would be the limit of our drug intake. Joe's recollection of an encounter with a punter after a particularly potent gig in the Western Counties on Praed Street is pertinent:

"...and he's winking and nudging me and I'm thinking `what's the matter with this geezer?' and the punter says `How many lines did you snort before that set then?`"

'"But we weren't into speed. We couldn't afford speed. We couldn't afford a drink! "

And I could hardly afford to replace my broken sticks. I would go down regularly to Foote's drum store in Golden Square because they'd have special boxes for used sticks and odd pairs. I'd just roll them out on the counter to make sure they weren't bent, and be happy to have a cheap supply.

*

Joe and I had become close friends. Not only were we brothers-at-arms so to speak in the regular scraps with our musical instruments, but we were both in love with a Piranha sister each, which of course brought us on to common ground. We shared some great times, like the occasion earlier in the spring when we had decided to make the most of an Easter break, and commandeered the hearse for a few days out in the sticks. We wanted to show our Spanish girls some Gaelic mountains, and so headed up North having adapted the hearse to sleep the four of us in the back. All was fine until the radiator sprang a leak somewhere in the Black Country. From then on we were condemned to filling up with water every fifty miles or so, but it didn't spoil the jaunt. We decided to break the journey to Snowdonia half way, and called in on some friends near to Leek in Staffs. Basford Hall was an imposing, rather spooky old Victorian country house, perched on a hill in its own acres, overlooking the beautiful Churnet valley. The owner had converted part of it into various large and very cold flats which had quickly been rented by friends as an interesting alternative to the normal place you could rent in town. Many a wild party had been held within its walls, and the night our hearse slid up the drive through the moorland mists was to be one of them. We left bleary eyed the following morning having hardly slept, which was not the case of a certain fellow reveller, the incredible Tarkus, who had somehow managed to crash out with no less than, rumour had it, ten tabs of acid circulating round his brain.

An unwelcome interruption to a night's sleep...

We purred on through the Welsh borders, to a little idyll on the Lleyn Peninsula; made sandcastles and love; watched dolphins out in the estuary, and all too soon re-took the road back to London. We had a rude awakening one night while parked up by the side of the road. Some superstitious person hadn't taken kindly to having a hearse outside their house and had called the police. Imagine, the four of us packed on to a double mattress in the back of the vehicle, being woken up and told to move on at four in the morning: guilty, your honour, of sleeping in a hearse on a public highway.

Meanwhile back in the smoke and by early July the situation in 101 was looking uncertain. The GLC was flexing its muscles and the future of the Walterton Road squats was in question. Then we heard of a possible squat down nearer to Portobello Road and we decided to check it out. But before that event Jules came up with another gig, also down the West End, that on the face of it looked very attractive. Ronnie Scott's was of course the most famous jazz club in the country. Some bright spark hit on the idea to cash in on its good name, and got the franchise to run "Rock nights" in a room above the jazz club: "Upstairs at Ronnie's". It was in fact a bit of a scam. They paid a real pittance to the bands, made a load on the bar, and thank you, next please..., but again we managed to salvage an interesting extra from the gig.

Radio Concorde was an underground pirate broadcaster operating in London at the time. As you would expect, they were well connected with the squatting fraternity, and they approached us with the idea of recording a gig to transmit at a later date. Live transmissions were of course out of the question. They had a running battle with the Post Office who had a monitoring section whose sole job was to control "illegal" broadcasting. On picking up a pirate signal they would send out "spotter" vans equipped with gear that could pinpoint the source. The police would then be called in, and a bust would be made if the station could be caught red-handed. This of course could be disastrous. Not only was there a possibility of a heavy fine, but also the valuable equipment would be confiscated.

We agreed to record the gig Upstairs at Ronnie's to be transmitted later from 101. What a laugh that was. They set up the aerial on the roof with the transmitter in an upstairs room. We acted as lookouts and stationed ourselves in various buildings and on street corners in the neighbourhood. Communication between us was difficult, this being, needless to say, before the era of mobile telephones. Sure enough the spotter vans suddenly appeared, but we got a message to the Radio in time for them to make their escape. Their scramble over the roof to a "safe" house further up the Road had been planned before hand, and although the broadcast was cut short, at least they didn't have their gear taken away. This, however, is precisely what happened to them a few months later, and we played a benefit gig in Hampstead Town Hall to raise funds for its replacement, sharing the bill there with Bonzo Dog, Viv Stanshall.

Woody, Esperanza and Paloma on the hearse in N. Wales.

The efforts of Jules and Mickey on the gig hunting front started to show results, and during the first couple of weeks of July we played no less than nine venues around London including pubs, benefits, and colleges. However, the doubts concerning our housing situation had to be cleared up, and we had to make a quick decision on whether to go for the new squat or not. In mid-July we decided to make the move.

Chapter 5   Stretching Wings

The house that we had our eyes on was a large, end of terrace abode, in the hands of a local housing association. We had heard about it through the afore mentioned "Ruff Tuff Cream Puff Estate Agency", the squatters organization that gestetnered lists of available property, and generally helped people that were looking for a place to live. The entry read as follows:

36 St Luke's Road. Empty two years. Entry through rear. No roof. Suit astronomer.

Sometimes information was a little inaccurate. In fact the house did have a roof, but as there was no astronomer among our ranks no one was disappointed. The fact that it was owned by a housing association meant there was always the faint possibility of us being able to negotiate with them once we were in, and work out some kind of deal. If that didn't happen then we could expect to hang in there for at least six months or so before they could sort out eviction orders, or maybe they would just let it ride.

From the outside it looked in great nick. There weren't any other squats in the street and it was unlikely to have had its installations smashed, not being a GLC house. The fact that there was a youth club in front on the opposite side of the road, and that it was the last house of a terrace meant that noise levels from the band room shouldn't cause too many problems. Having performed a previous reconnaissance, Simon, Esperanza and I went down armed with a new barrel for the lock, a jemmy and a screwdriver. We got in through the back and had a quick look through the house. It was perfect. All the services were connected; I think it even had a bath. All we had to do was change the barrel on the door-lock, and hide the evidence of our break in.

The police arrived just as we had finished changing the lock on the front door. Having the keys to the lock clinched it for us. We simply told them that we had just squatted the property and were now legal occupiers.

"...We got in through the back and had a quick look through the house..."

They could have gone looking for trouble and taken us down the nick on any number of charges – obstruction, conspiracy to cause criminal damage, going equipped for theft, forcible entry... but in the end I suppose they couldn't be bothered, and they just left us to it.

A couple of us stayed over that same night to consolidate the occupation, and over the next few days the others who had decided to make the change from 101 moved in. Apart from Esp and I, there were Big John, Joe and Paloma, Mickey, Rocco, Jules, and Mayumi, a Japanese friend. Round the corner from All Saints Road, five minutes from Portobello Road, the neighbourhood was livelier than Maida Hill, but all important was the fact that 36 St. Luke's Road had a large and easily sound-proofed front room in the basement. We had it all sorted out in a few days and the change didn't upset the momentum of the group.

It was like a breath of fresh air, and I remember feeling a renewed sense of purpose in the new rehearsal room. Mole, of course, was living round the corner just two minutes away and we would put in hours of playing together. Things were evolving in the song writing department. There was a greater elasticity, and with the new songs that Joe came up with at this time, we would attempt different feels, instead of treating them all as out and out rockers. Mole was, as I've mentioned, a great reggae fan, Clive was in to American bands such as Little Feat and Steely Dan, and Soul music had always been my favourite pop, so it was hardly surprising that at least we would try a funkier groove. "Hideaway" and "Green Love" had a cooler feel to them, whilst the treatment we applied to "Boo the Goose" was a shameless attempt at funking it up. Our unwritten acid test for any new song, however, was how it felt on stage, and it was difficult for anything that wasn't tearing at its leash to get our thumbs up. "Letsagatabitarockin" was just such a rocker, and in fact it was only on the menacing (but hardly pedestrian – paced) "Silent Telephone" that we would turn down the velocity dial a notch.

Meanwhile, a continuing stream of covers would be introduced to rehearsals, and remain or be discarded according to the same criteria as our original songs: Did they work live? I don't remember any arguing over what songs to leave in or kick out. If anyone had a strong opinion in either direction, then that would be enough. Mole had the great virtue of Bluntness. A spade was a spade to the Mole, and although his candour would get him in to rows, the value of an honest scowl over a "painted smile" requires no vindication. Clive, apart from his musical nouse, was a laid back easy going character and had a positive and level-headed influence in the group.

Joe was special. Even before the band had been started, he had that difficult to define characteristic that I suppose we call charisma. Its difficult to put your finger on exactly what it was. I think it stemmed from a real and genuine interest in all things and people around him. He had a very natural charm and ability to work with other people, and that special and endearing ability of leaders who know how to lead from within rather than from above. Although I'm sure he never claimed the title for himself (at least not with us present!), by now Joe had become undisputed, if undeclared, leader of the pack. Apart from his colossal commitment and the fact that all the new songs came from his pen, when it came to performance, he was the frontman and he was the persona with whom Joe Public would associate The 101'ers.

As for myself, I shared that commitment but was well aware of my severe limitations as a musician. How could I think otherwise with barely six months experience!? I was happy to take suggestions from my cohorts, but I really was limited in my technique, and the fact that our music was played at such speed didn't exactly help my endeavours to relax. I quickly realized that relaxation was the key to learning to play, to picking up new rhythms, and to gaining greater control over the instrument. I would rehearse every day on my own, and noticed an important fact. You could be trying ever so hard to achieve a new drum pattern to no avail, and then suddenly, when you weren't actually trying any more but rather off in some other place, suddenly Eureka, you would find yourself being able to play it! The lesson was clear: lots of practice and loosen up. The more I played drums the more I would be drawn to jazz. By this I don't mean that I wanted to be playing it in place of our music, it was just that for me jazz drummers were the tops. At the time (and come to think of it, at this time of writing as well!!) my favourites were Art Blakey and Philly Joe Jones, even more so than the then contemporary greats such as Tony Williams or Billy Cobham. Maybe it was because 50's and early 60's Bop drumming had a simpler more straight forward drive than later jazz. My other favourite, and certainly with a much greater direct relevance to the kind of music we were playing, was Al Jackson, the great Stax in-house drummer who played on most of the Memphis soul recordings, including the immortal Otis Redding sessions. Steady as a rock, almost understated, but for me King of the back beat.

To return to the band room, at this stage my contributions to the arranging of new songs during rehearsals certainly weren't that important, although as my experience increased, it would become more and more a facet of the group that I loved. Where I did feel more capacitated, however, was in the structuring of the set list and the general dynamics of the show, and Joe and I would invariably sit down before the gig and sort out the song order and write out the lists.

Gigs continued to come in throughout the summer. We really were gluttons for any possibility of playing. We went down to the Windsor Festival, with the venue changed from the Great Park to Watchfield, and actually played on each of the three different stages within an eight hour period! I can just imagine some glazed punter wandering half conscious around the festival site and speculating by the end of it all whether or not there had been any other band on the bill!

Meanwhile the Elgin went from strength to strength and it developed into a weekly haunt for Rockers from west London and further afield. Our audience was a pretty mixed bag. Often after the gig had finished and the pubs had shut any number of friends and fans would come round to St. Luke's. Joints would be fast flying round our front room, with booze picked up from the take away. One character that stands out in my memory from this time was Baker Barry. His mad stare, mumbled soliloquies, and disconcerting appearance with hair, eyebrows and eyelashes plastered with flour, could lead you to think he was one step from the loony bin, which in fact he probably was. But get him on the subject of R'n'B and you would be speaking to a mine of informed and interesting information. He had a huge collection of 40's and 50's blues and jazz, specializing in blues shouters and jump bands. I bought a few records from him, or maybe he gave them to me: a great, original

U.S. import of Count Basie in small band format, a rare recording of the San Antonio Ballbuster – Clarence "Gatemouth" Brown, Joe Turner, Louis Prima...

At The Elgin...dancing with a pint...

As for the band, we didn't slot into any of the more obvious urban tribes that were around in 1975. I've already mentioned that, despite the selection of our covers, traditional rock'n'rollers, Teds in other words, couldn't stomach our blitzkrieg versions. Peace and Lovers would be equally put-off by the nature of the music, and we were no way poseur enough for the glam rockers. Basically, we didn't look for any concrete image, and more or less dressed on stage in the same style as we would on the street. Being front man, Joe was more aware of this side of things, and got hold of a baggy, pinkish grey suit that he would usually accompany with a pair of grubby red trainers. I would wear the hat that I always wore anyway, at least until things got too hot under there for comfort. And that was just about the extent of our concession to fashion. We took pride in our independence, and "Squat Rock", "Beat Combo" or "A Rhythm & Blues Orchestra" seemed as good a labels as any for the various descriptions that we would put on ourselves. I remember an article in Time Out later that year referring to us as a Punk band, but I don't think any of us were hip enough to really know exactly what pigeon hole that was putting us into. If you push me, I suppose a Garage band is about the most accurate label you could put on us. As for being hippies, at the time we would have called such a description an irrelevance.... We had longish hair, someone might sport a beard now and then, maybe there were some flared trousers in our wardrobes, but at the time that was what you could pick up down the 'Bello or at some jumble sale.

At the beginning of August we played a couple of dates at the Hope and Anchor in Islington, and, along with the Nashville in West Kensington, the two pubs would become regular venues for us in the future. The Nashville gig stands out in my memory for the act we supported: The Troggs. Hard to forget a portly Reg Presley gyrating in his tight gold lame pants to the chords of "I Can't Control Myself". What I loved about him was the glint in his eye. He knew it was all just a bit ridiculous, but his attitude of "Bugger it.... I'm enjoying myself ...I'm getting paid... take it or leave it you lot.." was a fine lesson in authentic pop "non-attitude", as I prefer to call it.

I think it was at the second gig at the Hope that we first met, and under rather unfortunate circumstances, a fresh-faced young band up in London for their first gig in town. I was setting up my kit on stage, and down the stairs into the basement lurches another drummer with his hands full of cases.

"Sorry mate, first come and all that…"

Anyway the pub's posters and Time Out had us on the bill, so there was no argument really. The Hope's management, Dave Robinson, later co-founder of Stiff Records, had double booked The Jam and us. After the gig Robinson was to get further up my nose, as he looked askance at us and passed some derogatory comment as to our playing abilities, and that after a blistering set that brought the house down! A wily dog, he was no doubt checking us out, seeing if there was any mileage to be had out of this bunch…

It was around this time that Allan Jones put out a full feature on the band:

"…. They're young, arrogant, pretty crazed, with more energy than sense, and are just great… 'This is one that we found in our basement!' sneers Strummer, introducing one of his own tunes, "Motor Boys Motor". He dominates the centre of the stage fists clenched, his voice in a passionate embrace with the lyrics. Off to the left we have lead guitarist Clive W.H. Timperlee, who adds just the right amount of tasteful gloss to Strummer's demented chord thrashing. Drummer Snake Hips Dudanski, and Bassist The Mole, shore up the other end of the bicycle shed with a pile driving rhythm."

Getting a review like that was undoubtedly a big help. Micky Foote, as well as mixing the sound, had by now taken over managerial duties from Jules, and going armed with a decent press-cutting to a potential venue was often enough to clinch the gig. By the end of the summer we were also approached by a London based booking agency – Albion. It was of course on a non exclusive basis, and they were to be increasingly useful in finding dates for us. Meanwhile there had been developments on the domestic front.

*

I've talked about the problems of finding enough cash to live day to day, never mind the necessity of buying a new instrument or piece of sound equipment. Most of the earnings from gigs would go to pay group expenses – bits and bobs of P.A. gear being the prime culprit here, so taking on part-time work, combined with periods on the dole queue for Social Security, would be the usual solution, but there were of course other ruses which we would employ. Earlier that year, Joe had been able to buy himself a Fender Telecaster to supplant the cherry-red, semi acoustic Hoffner that had been his battle axe up until then. The money for this came from a scam that became relatively common, at least in our squatter circles at the time. A "marriage of convenience" would be mutually beneficial to both parties. In Joe's case the South African girl who he married received the benefits of British citizenship while he received the going rate, then round about 100 pounds. The only inconvenience might arise in the future when a divorce would become necessary, but that future seemed very far off in deed, and certainly not worth worrying about in the summer of 1975...

Immigration visas were a real problem for our Spanish friends. This was before Spain's entry into the European Community, and they were lucky to get a three month visitor's stamp at Heathrow, and had even more problems if they tried to get a job contract. Paloma couldn't of course walk down the aisle with Joe (he'd already married the South African), so she had to find a willing British bachelor. Similarly our Basque friend living in 101, Rocco also found an English rose to wed and solved his problem. That just left Esperanza.

What option did an English gent like me have but to ask for her hand in marriage? We made it all quite clear to our respective families. O.k., I was her friend and I wasn't charging her a 100 quid, but this was a purely bureaucratic formality ... we weren't really getting married ... just to cut out immigration problems for her.... definitely no presents thank you very much ... and no well-wishing hopes for a long and happy future. The ironies of life! Nearly forty years later, still together, and you start to think that maybe we should have accepted the odd box of cutlery.

I can't remember why we didn't use the hearse as our wedding carriage, it would have been a nice touch. We went down to Kensington registry office on the top deck of a 52 bus with some friends and Trouble the dog. Joe and Jeannie were our witnesses, but oops ... we'd forgotten to bring a ring. Never mind, Esp had one on her finger from a previous boyfriend. We whipped it off under the discreet gaze of the superintendent registrar, and signed, sealed, delivered that was that. I had actually phoned the Parks Department to make sure we would have no problems with officialdom, and we held our celebration near to The Spaniards, on Hampstead Heath. That Tea Room supplied the catering complete with a three tier wedding cake topped by an "Adults only" suspiciously brown looking tier on its summit. A somewhat limited selection of old 78's provided the music via an old wind-up gramophone with a huge horn, and a lethal concoction was of course available as liquid refreshment on this hot and sunny August afternoon. Staggering back to St. Luke's Road the festivities continued till the early hours, but not before the first occurrence of what was to become a permanent feature of our stay in St. Luke's: problems with the neighbours.

The "Metro" youth club in front of the house on the corner with Tavistock Road was used by kids from the area, and for a handful of them our house had become a potential target. During the party we found three or four lads (they were probably only in their mid teens) pinching stuff out of our rooms. There were nasty scenes as we ejected them, but having recognized them as from the club, we went over the following day to talk to the monitors. No joy there. They reckoned there were some uncontrollable elements and we'd just have to sort it out ourselves. The situation became a headache. It was easy for them to stake out the house, and especially when we were off playing somewhere there would be break-ins and general harassment of the place. We of course stepped up security in the basement with extra padlocks, fearing the day that we would come back to a band room with no gear for the band.

Paloma & Esperanza on the boat to Morrocco 1975

By the beginning of September we decided on a break. Where else but off to sunny Spain, after all there was a new son-in-law who had to pay his respects. We found the money for cheap flights down to Malaga and Esp, Paloma, Joe, and I headed off to Andalusia, not without considerable uneasiness over the security of our instruments in the basement. Problems back home were soon forgotten as we bathed in Spanish hospitality and the soothing waters of the Med. We decided on a quick visit to Africa, caught the bus down to Algeciras, hopped onto the ferry, and were suddenly plunged into the time warp of Morocco. We only had four or five days but we had some good larks experienced through an almost permanent zero-zero haze, before coming back recharged to face the music in West London.

The gear was still there, but only just. Sure enough, our friends from over the road had been back in to number 36, and living there was becoming intolerable. Mickey and Jules heard about a street that was being squatted only a mile or so away, up Westbourne Grove past Queensway, and went over to check it out. Perfect. Orsett Terrace was owned by the GLC and was in the same situation that Walterton Rd had been: one side recently refurbished while the other, our side-to-be, was awaiting redevelopment. Number 42, like our place in St Luke's Road, was the end house of a terrace, and had everything going for it. Various houses in the street had already been squatted and it was essential to move fast. Jules and Mickey got in through the basement (with Trouble tagging along), changed the front door lock and started clearing up the mess. Unfortunately for them, the police had been alerted and a pair in plain-clothes carted them off to Harrow Road nick, threatening to do them for criminal damage to a piece of corrugated iron. It was not until several hours later that they were released, the GLC having informed the police that they were not going to press charges. The council probably intended to get a court order when they were ready, to evict the whole street en bloc.

The rest of us went over to the new abode as soon as Micky and Jules were back with their story, and of course the keys to the front door. It was just what we were looking for. The house was huge, the services were on, and it was in good condition - you could even pull a handle in the rooms above and a bell would ring in the servant's quarters below, indicating the room in which services were required! But the very night that most of us were having a first time look around the Orsett Terrace house, the Youth Club was paying yet another uninvited visit to the house in St. Luke's. They had picked up a couple of cameras and a hi-fi and then decided to break down the locked door of a remaining room. Unfortunately for them, however, there was a girl temporarily staying in that room who was working in a local take away café. She recognized a couple of the lads, and screamed at them to leave the gear they had nicked, or else she'd be straight down to the police station. She must have put the fear of God in them. Incredibly they dropped the lot and left in a hurry. We got back later that night and Joe and I went round to the café with the vague hope of finding them, but it was no good, and anyway it wasn't now worth spending too much time on it. St Luke's was in the past, and it took us two or three days to move everything out.

Being owned by the GLC, the new house was likely to last a good few months, so we set about its organization. There were no shortage of rooms, which meant that everyone from St. Luke's could come in plus Jeannie (who had been with us in Walterton Rd), and the Mole. In the basement there was a rudimentary kitchen, and a large living room. True to "Squatting tradition" the first to occupy the house, in this case Mickey and Jules, had first option on rooms. Mickey had the room at the front on the ground floor, which doubled as an office, and in where we actually managed to install an increasingly necessary pay-phone. Other rooms were subsequently claimed on the same first come basis, so it was worth getting your claim in as quick as you could.

The band room was also on the ground floor at the back, which was ideal, as it meant we didn't have steps to haul the gear up and down. With the amount of gigs we were starting to play each week, this was becoming an important consideration. There were no close neighbours out at the back, but of course we couldn't risk having problems in that direction, and used the sound-proofing materials we had brought over from St Luke's.

The house was a classic mid-Victorian building that would have been built in the housing boom that accompanied the construction of nearby Paddington station in the 1850's. It amazes me, the huge number of grand houses all over west London. When you consider that each house had been owned by just one family, plus the servants of course, it gives an idea of the wealth that was landing in at least some people's pockets during the hey-day of Britain's empire building years. Well, this place was now in our hands and with a bit of luck it would remain so for twelve months or so. It is a fact that all in all we were a pretty productive bunch. Jeannie was still involved in running That Tea Room, Jules was studying photography at college, Big John had joined a theatre group, the band was going full tilt, and we even managed to set up a pottery studio in one of the rooms. Esperanza had been attending evening classes of ceramics and drawing since arriving in the New Year. She and Paloma were then offered, out of the blue and for next to nothing, a perfectly working electric kiln. The problem was installing it, but this was solved by our friend Ian – an electromechanical wizard, from Leek in Staffs, like Jules and me. He found time from between his efforts at setting up his Avolites stage lighting company, to wire us up to the company head, and within days the Piranha sisters had a fully functioning workshop.

The kitchen, as in our other houses, was mostly a place for the brewing of innumerable pots of tea; we ate in cheap local cafés, and from the ubiquitous chip bar round the corner. The absence of a bath in the house was no problem, and as in previous squats we used public baths. Two minutes away we had the council run Porchester Hall, which as well as bath tubs and swimming pool, boasted the once sumptuous Turkish baths, although these were usually out of our price range at the time, which was a shame. Like our house they really were a remnant of a more magnificent past. As you walked into the Edwardian wood panelled ante-chamber, little old men in shabby white coats would show you to your private, curtained cubicle. Having been handed your towels and hung up your clothes, the first stop would probably be in one of the three graded dry heat rooms (the hottest almost unbearable) each with various resting couches. Then there were the steam rooms, the ornately tiled ice-cold plunge pool, and a massage as an extra if your pocket could afford it. There were no time restrictions so we would usually go for at least a three hour session, and it was best to take a book to keep yourself amused in the long spells you would pass in the dry heat chambers. For me, the most interesting facet of the institution was the clientele that frequented it. There were very distinct groups, each of which kept pretty much to themselves. Russians, Jews, Arabs, Greeks, sportsmen, gays, hoods, cops, you name it, practically the whole spectrum of Bayswater's cultural diversity was represented, even squatters.

You stumbled, knackered, up the marble steps after even a final cold dip hadn't succeeded in reviving you, and the faded luxury still hadn't quite ended. Flopping out on your bed for a nap, you could ask one of the ancient attendants to wake you in forty minutes with a tray of poached eggs on toast and a cup of tea. Very civilized indeed. Meanwhile, at a corner table beneath a cloud of cigar smoke, a hushed huddle of maybe local masons would be finishing their game of poker.

*

As for the music, by now we really were beginning to believe that things were going somewhere. From now on gigs were never in short supply. Various pubs were becoming regular dates for us: Dingwalls, the Nashville, Hope and Anchor, and the Red Cow, apart from the Elgin which had become almost a home from home. It's interesting to reflect on the "pub rock" label that was later to be applied to the band. Of course we were playing pubs, along with college gigs, squatter and other benefits, festivals, you name it … we would play it, but I know that at least from my point of view I never consciously thought of ourselves as part of a pub rock scene. In fact I doubt if any other of the bands playing around at the time thought they were either. The whole concept of "Pub Rock" had more relevance as a journalistic tag, especially useful in a retrospective view from the later seventies, and of course it didn't apply to any particular type of music because basically there were bands in the pubs playing just about every style you could imagine: from country to reggae, from soul to glam, and from folk to manic rock, which is where we came in. The pubs were just a simple fact of life. For a band without a record contract it was a straight choice – you either stayed at home and played to your belly button's delight, or you grabbed any gig that was going, and luckily for us in London there were enough live music pubs to flood the Earls Court arena with rivers of best bitter.

On the contrary, rather than the sensation of belonging to a "scene", I remember feeling distinctly as if we were a bunch of outsiders. This would be especially so when one of our support slots would match us with an established and more accomplished band, like say Be-Bop Delux who we supported at North London Poly. This feeling of being separate and apart from the general current of other bands wasn't, needless to say, rooted in a feeling of inferiority. Far from it. It gave us a strong idea of our own identity, and usually the feeling would be: "OK they can play their licks better than us, but aren't they a load of boring bollocks…."

Richard, Joe & Trouble

Of course there were other groups in more or less the same line of business as us. The agency Albion had us booked in to the Nashville for a series of gigs sharing the bill with Eddie and the Hot Rods. They were another high octane outfit, based in Dr. Feelgood territory out in Essex. We would alternate sharing the headline spot with them, although that became an arrangement that quickly soured. Apart from their deranged harp blower, Lew Lewis, we didn't think too much of them, especially when they also started doing an extended version of "Gloria".

We played a gig as part of the Hope and Anchor Festival towards the end of October, and received a review in the New Musical Express much in the same vein as Jones's previously quoted piece for the M.M.

Chas de Whalley wrote:

- *" In the face of everything, including the humour of Neil Inness's Fatso, and Alberto y los Trios Paranoias, despite the massed vocal of J.B.'s Little Acre who were down in London for their first gig out of the Birmingham area, The 101'ers still emerged as the most outstanding band of the festival. They were so real it hurt. Every other band that played the Hope'n'Anchor Festival can blow the 101'ers off the stage when you measure them musically, of that there is not the slightest doubt. But those other guys are all experienced players, all been on stage before, all know what performing is all about....The 101'ers don't. On stage they break every rule in the book, because nobody's taught them how to read. Everything is so new and exhilarating, and they communicate that excitement to the audience."*

I must confess, because its beginning to niggle my conscience. Its three times now that I have quoted the London-based music press with reviews of the band; that same music press that, whilst recognizing its usefulness in promo for the band, I held in no small amount of disregard. You'll have to excuse me, but I'm afraid it's the only third party viewpoint I can find to corroborate the broad lines of this tale. God forbid, you might start thinking I'm inventing all this. Besides, I think I'm right in saying Allan Jones was a genuine fan of our music, and an unashamed promoter of "squat rock – proto punk" before punk became the darling of the press a year later.

And while we are on the subject of confession I also have to admit to another sensation that was fast becoming fact: increasingly I couldn't give a monkey's for the opinion of Joe Public in the audience. It didn't go as far as contempt for them, but as far as I was concerned the punters could take us or leave us. Perhaps it was normal rock syndrome egotism. Maybe it was also the result of a gradual build-up in the defences of a relatively incompetent musician. Definitely, it was a product of the monomania obsession that had developed, the mania being, of course, The 101'ers. When the audience were the faded stars and rock biz hang-er-on-ers that made up the Speakeasy clientele, the feeling was of total disdain. We would rattle through the set, get paid and get out.

Much has been made of the dire state into which rock had sunk by the mid 70's, due to the preponderance of a mega band culture out of touch with the kid in the street etc, etc... I don't think its quite as simple as that. You had Harley's Cockney Rebel in the charts, teenyboppers were tearing their hair out for the awful Bay City Rollers and the horrible Osmonds, but yes, rock was in general dominated by an elite largely hanging over from their 60's heyday, and there was an indefinable something in the air auguring change.

So, by the autumn of '75 there was the beginning of a rumble in the music press, and certainly a growing interest on the part of the punters, in the music we were playing, or maybe more so in our approach to it. But in '75, while its attraction lay essentially in its blend of untutored wild abandon, we were also well aware of a necessity for just the right amount of musicality to carry the whole thing off. It was exactly this balance that was to become the critical question for the band as '76 progressed, but for the time being we represented what was later dubbed as "an advance raiding party on the rock establishment" when put in the context of what was to become the full-blown punk explosion that was just around the corner.

Within the group there were developments on various fronts. Throughout the summer, one of our "guests" who appeared at the Elgin was "Desperate" Dan Kelleher. An old friend of Clive, at the time he was (or had been) playing bass with the Derelicts, the Squat Rock band from Latimer Road-way, who had first introduced us to the Elgin. By the autumn, these collaborations became a more permanent feature, and Dan would spend more time with us in rehearsals. He was without doubt a very talented musician. Keyboards, bass, guitar, drums, singing, composition, you name it and Dan could do it. He was also a Beatles freak, and could have won a Paul McCartney singing doubles competition hands down.

For the time being though he maintained a discreet profile in the band room, and contributed tasteful guitar on a song or two at live gigs.

On the management side of things, Mickey was hard pressed to handle all the organization, plus the sound, and especially the setting up at gigs. John "Boogie" Tiberi was a regular in the audience at the Elgin, and we accepted his offer to lend a hand. Later he got more involved in the logistics, but to start with he would help with the humping, keep an eye on the stage and sort out the monitor sound, while Mickey did the house PA. He also had a useful contact with a rich lady with spare cash. We had been using our original, antiquated PA system from the early days, but it really wasn't up to handling a room of any size never mind a hall, and some of the gigs we were now getting required more powerful and better quality equipment. His friend lent us the money – "just like that", and we set ourselves up with a nice bit of gear, probably only about a 1Kw rig with some decent mikes, but for us it was a gift from heaven. It made a big difference, especially having monitors so that you could actually get a half decent sound on stage and hear at least something of what the others were playing.

Other changes were in the transport department. The hearse just wasn't big enough any more for carting the gear around to the venues, and besides, Big John could make good use of it in the comedy theatre group that he formed. Dave the Van Driver, a dance floor fanatic from the early days of the band, took over all haulage duties within a reasonable radius of London, and his beaten up Bedford didn't fail us over the following months. Nothing was ever too much trouble for Dave the V.D., although for gigs out of town we would hire a self-drive rather than risk his van.

The days shortened and winter's murk descended on our west London patch, but before the changes that were to accompany the coming of '76, we had a call one morning that sent a buzz up through the floors of nº 42. Someone wanted to put us into a recording studio.

Chapter 6   Barbed Wire Blues

That someone was Vic Maile, and the fact that his name was known to us as producer of the first Dr Feelgood album "Down by the Jetty", meant no questions asked as we eagerly loaded up the van and shot up to a modestly equipped eight track facility, Jackson's Studio in Rickmansworth. Ok, it wasn't a record deal, but it was an exciting development. Apart from Clive, none of us had ever been inside a studio before, and here was a respected producer offering us the chance.

The deal was straightforward enough. It didn't cost us anything, and Jackson's retained the copyright, leaving us at the very least with a studio quality demo. Vic had been in the sound biz for years, his live recordings including discs by The Who and Led Zeppelin from the early 70's, and using the Rickmansworth studio he was starting to record young bands that caught his fancy. The Canvey Isle connection between Dr. Feelgood and the Rods meant that he had probably seen us at a Nashville gig with The Hot Rods who he was also recording.

The man had a very retiring manner. Whether from shyness, boredom, or aloofness, I am not quite sure, but it was clear that he wasn't there for messing around, and he knew exactly what he wanted to do and how to get it. I can't remember how we selected the songs to record, very strange that Keys to Your Heart was not amongst them. Maybe the title put Vic off, he was very much the hard rocker! We recorded just about our full repertory of self penned songs: Sweety, Motor, Silent Telephone, Steamguage 99, Letsagetabitorockin', and Hideaway, a newish song at the time.

To rattle off six songs in an afternoon wasn't bad going, down of course to a no-nonsense production technique. Once the drum sound was sorted, it was a question of up and away with a maximum of three takes per song. Always a good policy as far as I as a drummer was concerned, the original freshness of a performance paling after the first couple of takes of a song. We recorded the songs virtually live, with a guide lead vocal that of course Vic was not averse to using if it was good enough. There might have been a couple of lead guitar overdubs, a tambourine on Steamguage, and that was it.

Packed up and out five hours later, I remember feeling content with our efforts, and especially when we received a copy of the final mix that Vic ran off a couple of days later. Maile's recording had no greater pretension than a "warts an' all" demo, but even that was light years ahead of the previous recordings we had made on cassette from the rehearsal studio, or from live gigs - whether on Mickey's ever turning cassette machine or a revox such as was used for the Radio Concorde broadcast. However, my feelings on the matter weren't shared by all. Mole hadn't got on at all with Vic, and he thought the session had been a wasted opportunity. Well, he might have had a point. Maybe we should have concentrated on two or three songs instead of six, maybe we should have had a re-look at the arrangements, or spent more time on overdubs, but at the end of the day we were very much the green-horns with Vic calling the shots.

There was no immediate outcome from the recordings. Presumably the production company played them to United Artists or other labels with which they had contacts, or maybe Vic thought they weren't up to public scrutiny! We used the tracks as a demo when hunting for gigs, and they were then quickly forgotten until surfacing on vinyl at a much later date.

The band carried on with its busy schedule of live dates. Increasingly gigs as headliners or as support for the likes of Jess Roden, Mickey Jupp, Pirate Green's Shanghai, Ian Dury and the Kilburns, or Nelson's Be-Bop Deluxe necessitated the hiring of a Transit and forays along the highways and byways of the Kingdom. Sheffield, Manchester, Hereford, Derby were all visited towards the end of the year, and of course all was done on a shoe string budget. We couldn't afford bed and breakfasts, never mind a hotel, so with luck we would avail ourselves of the offer of a sleeping bag on a friend's floor, or face the long haul back to London after the gig.

Mickey at the controls…

Back home, life in Orsett Terrace had never a dull moment. Our side of the street had quickly filled up with squatters: about twelve houses, with a population of all shapes and sizes. We had less to do with the other houses than during our time in Walterton Rd, probably due to the fact that we had little time between gigs and rehearsals, but through Esperanza and Paloma we quickly got to know our immediate neighbours in number 40. It was a Spanish house, with a group of friends and family mostly from Madrid. Juanma and Carmen were both avid rockers, and they became close friends as well as keen followers of the 101'ers. Many an evening would be spent in their top floor room, sharing a fine Spanish brandy and the latest Moroccan treat. Juanma would sit in his low arm-chair, his prominent fore-head, sharp aquiline profile and exquisite Spanish manners lending him an almost regal demeanour. Joe was quick to dub him "The King of Spain".

King and Queen were to receive an unwanted surprise one winter's night. It started to rain heavily, and within minutes of the downpour starting there was water literally pouring in torrents through the ceiling in to their rooms. Next morning we went up through a trap-door on to their roof. The explanation for the previous night's disaster was clear. All the lead flashing from the roof had disappeared; a classic case of British roof-stripping, the lead being taken off for sale to a scrap metal merchant.

Juanma and Carmen were left with the costly and urgent problem of sorting out their roof before the next downpour came. We in 42 were left thinking that we would probably be next on the hit-list. Our terrace of houses were all connected, and access from one roof to another was easy, so it was reasonable to assume that the culprits had climbed out on to the roof-tops from one of the houses up the road and simply walked along until they had come to something that took their fancy. Preventive action on our part was not easy to invent. The following day I called in to the ironmongers on Queensway and bought a roll of barbed-wire. We grappled with a hastily knocked-together wooden frame and strung up the wire defences across the access to our roof. It was no great surprise, however, when a few days later a rehearsal was interrupted by an excited call from Simon who had a room on the top floor of our house. He thought he had heard noises from above, so a couple of us raced round to next door, and came up through the hatch door of number 40, hoping to be able to catch the lead thieves red handed. However, they must have realised that we were on to them and scarpered quickly, although the evidence was there of them having tried to wrench off the lead flashings. So much for our First World War style defence system.

Questions asked among our various neighbours led to suspicion falling pretty heavily upon a certain junky occupied house several doors up the terrace. Big John then came up with a brilliant idea. The simple solution was to walk along the roof tops until we came to the suspect house; drive half a dozen six inch nails through the trap door and its frame, thus making it impossible for anyone to use the roof exit from that house; and wait to see if we had put our finger on the guilty party. No more lead was taken, so presumably we had guessed right as to the offending abode.

From investigators to investigated, our role was reversed a couple of weeks later. One late afternoon we were taking a five minute break from rehearsals in the large kitchen-living room in the basement of the house. There was a crowd of us in there having a quick cuppa and a smoke when we were interrupted by a loud rap on the basement door. I opened up to a special branch cop flashing his ID at me and making it quite clear that he was coming in whether I liked it or not. My immediate alarm at thinking we were in for a drug bust was soon allayed. He didn't bat an eyelid as he entered a living room wreathed in a pall of ganja smoke, had a look round, and suggested I accompany him on a tour of the house. We went through every room in the place, and it was clear that he knew exactly what he was looking for, and it was not drugs. Whatever it was, he didn't find it, and twenty minutes later he left as mysteriously as he had arrived.

We were left thinking what the hell was all that was about, and came to the conclusion that he was probably from the Bomb Squad. There had been three or more different bombs planted in London by the provisional IRA in the autumn of '75, and as was later to come out in the Guilford Pub Bombing framing affair, the squatting community was a target for anti-terrorist investigation.

*

There was, however, a smouldering fuse present in the 101'ers that led to an unfortunate explosion one day in mid January. Joe and I had to make a very unpleasant decision. Having convinced ourselves of its necessity, we slouched off to the Mole's den in Tavistock Road on a cold and drizzly Night of the Long Knives. Our close friendship with Mole at least stimulated us into delivering the news personally. We had decided that it was the end of the 101'ers for Mole.

"We've no choice in the matter".... "You don't seem happy with the band anyway", all our reasoning seemed pretty flimsy, confronted with the look of hurt and betrayal on our friend's face. The hatchet job done, we were relieved to duck out of his house and make our way back home across Westbourne Park, depressed with the affair, but no doubt thinking that for the band the best decision had been made. I am not so sure now.

What is true is that, from when Dan had started to collaborate with us, Mole had become more and more difficult to work with. Irascible at the best of times and prone to the blackest of moods, he could be very difficult to handle, and with Clive the relationship was cool when at its best. It must have been pretty obvious to Mole that the newcomer Dan was becoming a potential threat to his position in the group, Dan being a good friend of Clive and a very fine musician. Mole's insecurity grew at a par with Dan's increased input to the band, and eventually the tension in rehearsals arrived at the point where something had to change. Given the state Mole was in we did not really have much option, but it was a very sad affair. Here were Joe and I giving the chop not only to our friend, but also to someone who could play his instrument at least as well as we could, and on top of that to someone who was 100% committed to the band. But most important of all, Mole was a survivor of that difficult to define "feeling" that had characterized the beginnings of the group. What we were to gain from a greater professionalism, we certainly lost in terms of "mad spirit". Six months later the same dilemma might well have produced a different decision, but that, of course, is something we will never know...

Shortly afterwards Mole came down to a gig we had booked at a London college. I wonder what went through his mind as he watched us from in front of the stage. I hope that he felt at least just a touch of relief to offset the bitterness. He did not stay till the end of the set.

Despite the fact that Dan had been guesting on guitar for some time, he had a tall order over the next couple of weeks. We had no less than twelve dates to play in fifteen days. London gigs included a support spot at The Roundhouse in Chalk Farm, a trip up to Birmingham and another to Halifax, Sheffield, and Scunthorpe. There were no problems, though, and he was well settled in by the end of that time.

*

So now, once again, the air in the band room was cleared, and we set about reorganizing with Dan. Apart from his experience and dexterity on bass, he had other skills to offer. The backing vocals was one area that immediately improved with not just his singing but also with the harmony parts that he arranged, and then there were two or three songs on which he sang lead vocal, which would give Joe a welcome breather at strategic points in the set. He also helped me in working out new drum patterns. One of the first songs I remember doing with him was a cover that Joe had brought to a rehearsal. "Junco Partner" was an early 50's recording by James Wayne. A classic New Orleans piano blues about a down and out jailbird, once in the set it was never to leave, and along with Gloria it became just about my favourite cover. Dan suggested a gumbo influenced beat for the song that I just loved to play, and we started going through all the songs, generally tightening things up and looking at the bass drum – bass guitar interplay.

But where Dan's experience really came through was in the arrangements for the new songs that were introduced over the next few weeks. "Rabies From the Dogs of Love", "Five Star R'n'R", and "Sweet Revenge" were all songs penned by Joe around this time, and put through the mill during rehearsals. The first two were pretty much in our normal up-tempo vein, whilst the latter was the nearest we ever came to creating a ballad with its loose, country-calypso feel. For me, these latest songs represented a distinct progression from their predecessors, and the fruit of the experience gained over the previous year began to show. We certainly did not change the general tone of the band, but there was just a touch more sophistication to the arrangements. As far as I was concerned, I would look to incorporate new rhythms and patterns in to my playing. In "Five Star", for example, there was a long break in the middle into which I introduced an up - tempo latin feel, and in "Rabies" a couple of middle-eights where I crossed into a counter rhythm on the toms to accompany the "Help me doctor" chorus. Small details perhaps, but for me they were very important. It was really a question of pushing my abilities to their limits, even if it meant trying new things that were only half mastered.

Joe's writing was of course also developing, the lyrics taking on more and more of his individual stamp. As he once introduced it at a concert (albeit with very pronounced tongue in cheek), "Rabies" was a "social message" song, to help stop the spread of the "love disease".

"Let me see you down ....Help me doctor, help me doctor
On your knees .... Help me doctor, help me ...
Only takes a minute ..... Help me doctor, help me...
At the Praed Street Clinic "

where the Praed Street clinic refered to a venereal disease unit in Paddington, visited by all of us at one time or another!

Of all the songs Joe wrote with us, the lyrics of "Sweet Revenge" are perhaps my favourite. A plaintive melody and a more laid back tempo allowed for more expression in the singing, which particularly suited the subject. Contrary to what the title suggests, revenge is rarely sweet:

"Sweet Revenge.....
She carries a bitter sting
You go around believing in her
But she don't bring a thing..."

Far from any macho rock strutting, Joe would admit that:
"Any stain upon the floor,
The blood was always mine".

So, after the stormy last few weeks with Mole, things were looking good. The live gigs were better than ever, and there was a new creative impulse in the band room.

Ted...

Chapter 7 Devils in the Chapel

When Dan had made his debut with us on bass at the London college gig in mid January, as I said, Mole hadn't waited around till the end. However, into the dressing room after the show came two characters with familiar faces and a very interesting proposition. Ted Carroll and Roger Armstrong ran a couple of record stores which were well known to us, especially the Rock On stall in a covered part of the Golborne Road market. There you could browse through one of the best collections of non mainstream rock in town, specializing in 50's R'n'R and rockabilly, off- beat U.S. garage bands, northern soul, and R'n'B.

Their idea was simple: they wanted to sign us for a one off single deal on their newly created label, Chiswick Records, and of course we jumped at it. We had heard no positive news from Vic Maile since our session with him at Jackson's, and of course the possibility of bringing something out on vinyl was right on top of our agenda.

The fact that Chiswick was a virtually unknown label, with just one previous release to its credit did not lessen the excitement. Prior to the punk explosion that was just around the corner, new bands in our situation would find it extremely difficult to land a record deal, even for a one-off single. The whole recording industry was sewn up by the major companies, and as I've already commented, the industry was very much out of touch and uninterested in new currents, and brash young bands. The nearest you came to independents were Virgin and maybe Island, but of course they were really in the same league as CBS, Polydor and the rest of the multinationals.

Chiswick took their cue from the U.S. and Jamaican independents like the Stax, King, and Blue Beat labels. Being, as it were, on the street, they were perfectly placed for the changes that were to occur in the structure of the music industry over the next couple of years, and indeed were key players in that transformation. They were probably the first truly independent and influential rock label to surface in the mid seventies, and though they never achieved the commercial success that came to some, they were the immediate precursors of labels such as Stiff, Rough Trade, Beggar's Banquet, Mute and a host of others.

We gave the go ahead there and then to the Chiswick offer, agreeing to finalize the details once we had completed the hectic gigging schedule of the following weeks. One of these dates included a gig at the Roundhouse, which was a good one to have, if only for the affection we felt towards the place, it having been one of London's main centres for alternative rock music culture since the mid 60's. However, through the promoter of this show, John Curd, we were to land a gig at an even more interesting venue, where of all the 101'ers' performances the images stand out clearest in my mind.

Wandsworth prison in South London is a top security establishment catering for long term guests of Her Majesty. One thousand three hundred male inmates incarcerated in a state-of-the-art prison: state-of-the-art, that is, in 1850 when it was built. We piled into Dave the VD's Bedford and rattled off south of the river not knowing really what to expect. First stop was a small door in a huge stone turreted wall, towering above us like the battlements of Macbeth's castle. A sneering officer answered our ring at the bell with a not too friendly welcome. Yes, they were expecting a musical ensemble that morning, but:

"Sorry gentlemen, definitely no dogs or females allowed in 'ere, thank you very much."

Jeannie and the Piranha sisters had to turn on their heels and take the Pig Dog for a long walk on Wandsworth common. The gates cranked open, we were directed to a door for unloading, and we proceeded to hump the gear under the very attentive eyes of a couple of screws and their inquisitive hound. It was just as well Trouble hadn't been allowed in: the police dog looked as though he'd have eaten him alive. A couple of oldish boys in prison greys and with ready smiles appeared from nowhere and helped us with the equipment. We learnt by degrees that the red arm-bands they wore designated them as "reliable inmates". From then on, all our contacts with officialdom were through them, and this included a continuous supply of weak tea and moldy biscuits.

We were led into a large circular domed chapel. Trust the Victorians to have endowed their institution with an enormous place of worship, so very concerned they would have been with the spiritual health of the condemned. So this was to be the site for our musical offering, and lo and behold – where else to erect the stage but over the altar on a raised dais at one end of the church. The sacristy, where the priest would have donned his vestments, was our dressing room, and the ironies were beginning to leave a wry smile on my face. As a ten year old I had seriously considered embracing a vocation to the priesthood, to devote myself to a life in the service of the Lord. Here I was pulling on my stage gear to partake in a very different kind of ritual. We had come prepared with a special liturgy for this particular ceremony, and our sacrificial offering contained as many prison-related songs as we could manage: Jailhouse Rock, Out of Time, Junco Partner, and a special rendition of Riot in Cell Block Number 9. Truth is, I think we were more nervous than we had ever been as we filed out on to the stage not knowing what kind of reception we would receive.

A complete and utter stony silence greeted us as we took to our instruments and Joe introduced the first song. I looked out from my drum stool and saw the chapel full to the brim, a sea of intent faces, five hundred or so inmates seated in their pews, the first row not two yards from us, with a ring of uniformed warders leaning nonchalantly against the back wall. It's a fact that we would give our all every time we performed, but at this gig we were determined to unload at least 101 per cent. After all, here we were a bunch of fresh-faced, squatter musos with all the freedom life could offer, playing to an audience some of whom had before them the stark reality of twenty years or more behind prison bars. How could we compare them to our normal college student punter, or Speakeasy sycophant? We tore into the first song like there was no tomorrow, and sure enough at its end the place erupted.

"...Order restored, they now remained seated, straining at their shackles and casting furtive glances at their keepers..."

They loved it, but there was something not quite right. As quickly as the clapping and cheering had started, it stopped. It dawned on me that of course here as well, the inmates were all very much under strict orders. The screws around the perimeter of the hall would suddenly make their presence felt after a minute's applause, and silence would once again descend on the chapel. No standing up either.

The set continued. Joe was in great form, and making the most of a continual battle with an unstable mike stand, he quickly established a rapport with the audience. I'll never forget the expressions on the faces in front of us. It's no exaggeration to describe most of them as ecstatic. Imagine being cooped up in that place day in and day out for years, and then suddenly being in front of a hot rock band firing on all cylinders. As song followed song some of the men became bolder. I don't know if it was because the keener rock fanatics had managed to get seats at the front, or because they were the furthest away from the guards mostly situated at the back, but the first rows were getting carried away, and you could see them unable to remain seated, hanging on every word, and not missing the smallest detail of what was happening. Towards the end of the set my bass drum pedal broke, which for Joe was yet another opportunity to have a chat. A repartee built up, and I remember shouts of "keep taking the tablets!" and other witticisms in response to Joe's quips, yet another mistaken assumption as to the source of our energy! At one point a couple of warders came down near to the front and made it clear what the limits were. Order restored, they now remained seated, straining at their shackles and casting furtive glances at their keepers when, maybe at the end of a song, they remembered where they were. A couple of encores and that was that. We would have carried on playing all day if it had been up to us, but the men in red arm bands made it clear that our time was up. I'm not sure at what point it was, but a suspicion gradually formed about these "trusted ones". Though prisoners, it was clear that they had special privileges, and you started to wonder exactly what they would have done to get them! By the time we had cooled off and changed, accompanied by yet more gallons of tea, rightly or wrongly, these willing helpers appeared in a different light. An unjust deduction perhaps, as of course we knew nothing of the inner workings of the place.

We loaded the van, again under the close observation of the guards – maybe they thought we could have had a prisoner hidden in the bass drum, or perhaps a pair of candlestick-holders in a guitar case, and trundled out of the main gate. As Clive would later wryly observe:

"There's nothing like a captive audience."

True indeed. For me it was the most enjoyable gig we ever performed.

*

We now had the recording session with Chiswick pencilled in for the beginning of March, but before that we had the by now usual string of dates to fulfil. The residency at the Elgin had finally come to an end in January, an apologetic landlord blaming his neighbours opposite the pub, who had apparently organized a petition complaining of excessive noise. We went down there one night and sure enough, were met by a fiddler and singer playing Irish ballads at a much reduced volume.

How things had changed for us over the previous twelve months. Either by our own efforts, or increasingly through the Albion agency, there was now no problem finding gigs. It was through the agent that we were booked up for our European tour. In fact it was nothing more than a long weekend Continental break, but eventful none the less. We hired a van, took the ferry over to Belgium and the same night were installed in a little hotel in downtown Amsterdam. The first show was at a club run by the hotel owner, the second in the could one say "legendary" Paradiso club, and the next in a dive down in Rotterdam. After the first two nights our opinions of a laid back boring hippy Holland were pretty much confirmed, but the third night in the Eksit Club was a revelation. Of all the places we ever played, this club I remember as the most violent. There was an underlying viciousness in the atmosphere, with ninety percent of the punters out of their heads on something or other. I remember one bloke leaning against the bar dropping one glass after another on the floor, presumably just to see it smash, with none of the bar staff blinking an eyelid. There were outbreaks of fighting in the audience, and a marked antagonism towards us. It was beginning to feel as if we were the unwilling participants in a Roman blood-lust Games, with the crowd just waiting with a wavering thumb to unleash the lions upon us. Joe, as usual, was not to be phased by all this, and gave back the verbal abuse as good as he was given.

We didn't hang around long after the set and headed off on the road to a small club in Ghent for the final night of the mini-tour. Again, it was a complete contrast to the previous night. This place almost achieved the giddy heights reached by Sweety's St. Moritz in terms of boredom and dubious punter appreciation, but was also to gain notoriety in our own personal agenda of "highs and lows" for another reason. We performed for the first and last time a version of the country classic "Jambalaya" by Hank Williams that completely fell apart at the seams. Whether it was the fault of the strong Belgium lager or not is debateable. It was an awful moment on stage and we were left gob-smacked, just staring at each other thinking what on earth was happening and waiting for the nightmare to finish. As far as I can remember it only occurred one other time. That was at one of the first gigs we had at the Nashville nine months or so previously, when we played a version of the Stones - Ry Cooder song "Memo from Turner". The same thing had happened. Everything at sixes and sevens – out of tune, out of time, and red faces. What a relief it was to finish it and crash into the next number.

On returning we had just a couple of days to sort ourselves out for the Chiswick session. We decided on our new material – "Sweet Revenge" and "Surf City". Also "Keys to Your Heart, the first song Joe had penned, but which for some strange reason we hadn't recorded with Vic a few months earlier. Roger Armstrong, who was to produce, had us booked in to Pathway Studios in Kentish Town. Even we were a trifle surprised at the size of the studio as we banged our gear through the front door. There was barely room for Roger and the engineer in the control room, and we squeezed the guitar amps and drum kit into a miniscule recording area. Not that we were complaining. We started the session with a great feeling of anticipation, and though you could no way describe it as relaxed, there was certainly a good natured atmosphere that had been missing during our previous bash with Vic. The engineer knew his studio and had the sound up within a couple of hours, and Roger just let us get on with playing our music in the way we were accustomed. He was very easy going, receiving other ideas as easily as he put out his own.

We decided to have a go at Surf City even though it was barely off the drawing board and hadn't yet entered the gig set lists. It was Dan's song, a bit of a spoof take on bubble gum surf music, but I remember Joe had a go at singing it. It didn't work out however, and neither did it when Dan took to the lead vocal. The other songs were a different story. We laid down rhythm tracks for "Keys" and "Sweet Revenge", the latter being tried with Clive on acoustic rather then electric guitar. A week later we were back in for another session and after another poor attempt at "Surf City" decided to put down our other new song at the time – "Rabies". Overdubs were again kept to a minimum. If I remember right, it was the first time Clive used a heavily distorted lead guitar on the song, and in the final bars we recorded a Boogie "Walking the dog" style whistle. I really can't remember all of what I thought of our efforts. However, I have a vague recollection of not being too happy with the version of "Keys". It was so much slower than our live versions, that I remember thinking it a trifle sluggish. I do remember that Joe had a heavy cold at the time. You can hear it in his voice, even more than usually rasping, especially in the version of "Sweet Revenge" that Chiswick were to release at a much later date, but for me it adds to its attraction. The recording completed, the tapes were left with Roger who was to mix them a couple of weeks later at Chalk Farm Studios, and as usual the band continued with its hectic schedule of dates.

The day after the final Pathway session we were on the road again. This time up to Nottingham, followed yet again by Sheffield, a spot at Samantha's in my home town Leek, and a show at Liverpool University which I remember for the great reception by a packed out hall. A couple of days off were then followed by another string of gigs including trips out to Scunthorpe, Colchester and High Wycombe, and another visit to Wandsworth nick, the inmates having apparently put in a special request for our return.

You might think we were starting to make a bit of money. Hardly. After paying for the van hire and other expenses practically all of the gig money would go to paying back money we owed for the PA system that had been bought with borrowed money. There was no way you could keep even a part time job going with the hectic schedule that we had and I think all of us were now signing on at the dole office. We would receive the minimum Social Security pay out, but this would be enough to keep up with the basics.

Towards the end of April we had yet another offer to record. This was a bit of a strange one, and came about through an old acquaintance of Clive – Mike Robinson, an engineer who worked in the BBC's Maida Vale sound facilities. He generously offered us the use of one of the studios, plus his services as engineer, and I think it was through Boogie that we roped in Simon Jeffes to help out in the production. Simon (Penguin Café Orchestra) fitted in from the word go, even though we'd never met him before. He put forward his ideas in his very discreet manner, and invariably we accepted his opinion.

The studio was by far the biggest and best equipped that we had been in, and the presence of a Hammond organ with its Leslie sitting in a corner, was quickly noted by Dan. Maybe the fact that it was only five minutes walk from 101 in Walterton Road, had something to do with it, but we felt very much at home in the place. Also perhaps we were starting to accustom ourselves to the recording process, so different from live gigs. We rattled off "Surf City", using the Hammond to good affect, and then put down "5 * Rock and Roll", another of the recent self-penned songs. Our decision to record another version of "Keys to Your Heart" was probably due to the fact that we weren't completely convinced of the track we'd just recorded at Pathway with Roger. Besides, our experience with the Jackson's sessions had taught us that a recording session doesn't necessarily result with vinyl in the shops. We were to also put down a backing track of "Rabies", thinking of the possibility of bringing something out on our own label, if the deal with Chiswick (for which there was still nothing signed) didn't happen.

Over the next couple of weeks, whenever spaces in our diary and that of Mike Robinson coincided, we would be in and out of the BBC, putting down overdubs and mixing, but the gigging schedule didn't let up. To take us up to the end of March we played two gigs of note. One down in Canterbury had been set up by the Albion agency where we were supported by a group called "The Stranglers". Not at all impressed with them, "gloom rock" was our general opinion. A couple of days later and we played a benefit for our friends from "That Tea Room" in Acklam Hall under the West Way, and shared the bill with Tymon Dogg. This was to be our last collaboration with Tymon, and the last gig before a certain show on the 3rd of April in the Nashville Rooms. We were booked in with a group unknown to us at the time. They were called "The Sex Pistols".

Chapter 8 Snot Rag and a Snarl

Although without doubt an oversimplification, I would say that in the process of writing a book such as this you find yourself working basically on two levels: firstly, setting out the bare factual details, and secondly the interpretation of those events. For the former, although I can't deny that the 'editing' of those facts is a totally biased process, you rely on your own memory of events and on written information such as can be found, for example, in the gig diary that Clive wrote at the time, or in relevant entries found on the web etc... However, for the second level of 'interpretation', all pretence at an 'objective' approach really is nothing more than that: a pretence. This little tale is of course a very subjective and personal account of 'what happened and why', and doubtless the other players in the story would and will have very different interpretations, even if we were to agree (a distinctly doubtful supposition) on all the basic facts of the case.

As a thirteen year old in art class at school, I remember trying to express this very strong feeling of what I suppose you could describe as an extreme subjective and relative view of the universe. A world where there are an infinite number of viewpoints from which to view the same occurrence, all giving a different view of the same phenomenon. I tried to describe it visually as a sphere, and for a metaphor I drew an orange, at the very core of which was the object under observation. My very poor artistic attempt looked rather like a fly's 'compound' eye under a microscope. A 'viewpoint' could be taken from any point on the circumference of the sphere (the orange peel in my case) looking inwards towards the core. The appearance of the 'phenomenon' would obviously vary depending upon the point on the orange peel from which you were looking. In fact there would be an infinite number of takes on the same object: 360° by 360°, each with a different view of the point under observation. I am no mathematician, but I think that makes sense?!

So, I can assure you that I am well aware that my interpretation of the events which I shared and experienced with others back in the mid 1970's (and of course in the rest of this tale) is no doubt open to a myriad of other interpretations. This doesn't mean that it lessens the validity of my opinion, or that I doubt unduly my own interpretations, but it is a sobering thought. It also tempers my inclination to criticise, especially given the fact that the other party isn't actually here to put his/her viewpoint.

This little philosophical preamble is leading to one important observation. Until now in the story of this group I have for the most part been happy to use indistinguishably the words 'I' and 'we'. This story is my story of a group, a band, a musical ensemble; and a group by definition is a plural entity where there is at least a minimum of common identity between the members. From now on in the tale this common identity would slowly but surely start to fragment. From now on I can hardly use the 'we'; it has to be the 'me', and 'him' or 'them'.

From the first minute of contact with this new group that had been booked to support us, there was the feeling that this was no ordinary band, and that in itself, in the world of pop music, is saying a lot. Of course each of the four of us reacted to the Pistols 'experience' in his own way. My reaction was mixed. Musically I liked them. I liked the songs they played and I liked the sound they generated. I also liked the feeling they put in and the attitude they had, which wasn't so dissimilar to the early days of our band. In fact at this first gig we got on fine with them, chatting about this and that in the dressing room; an all right bunch of geezers you might say. But there were two aspects to it that didn't impress me at all, and they had nothing to do with the group on the stage. The first was the guy who was orchestrating everything that they would do. Looking at them with arched eyebrows like a schoolmaster with his pupils; asking if they wanted this, telling them to do that. There was no disputing who was boss in that outfit, at least at this early stage in their life. Second, was the crew of fans that they brought down with them. A right bunch of poseurs is what I thought, just so incredibly self-conscious and supercilious. Wouldn't deign to cross a word with you if you weren't part of their little clique and dressed in the right clothes, which looked pretty damn expensive to me in any case.

a bored looking crew...

But what was not to be denied was that here was evidence of something that at least Joe and I had been talking of and dreaming of for months. Here was the germ of something new, young and definitely different. Could it be that the feeling that had been in the air for at least the previous 12 months - that it was time for a shake up and a change in the status quo, was taking shape before our eyes? Maybe, but I for one didn't like certain aspects of its shape! There were hints of a cynical negativity with an underlying current of posed violence, it was exclusive and it was highly manipulated. But of course, I was a fool. Any new scene was bound to be manipulated by someone, was bound to take an extreme identity, with black and white, oversimplified answers. All this was just glimpsed at during that first gig at the Nashville.

Others in our group had their own reactions. Clive and Dan were pretty much dismissive, but Joe was taken with them. The 'Paul on the road to Damascus theory' of instant conversion has its attraction for describing Joe's reaction to the Sex Pistols, and he himself would later interpret the events along such lines, but at the time I don't think the process was quite so simple. There is no doubt, however, that our first contact with the Pistols had left a very strong impression. He was later to say that what really grabbed him had been their attitude:

- "We're goin' to play this and if you don't like it you can stuff it, 'cos we're playing it anyway!"

He was to contrast this with our supposed attitude.

"Hope you enjoy our next tune".

I don't think that's anywhere near a true description of the attitude he or the rest of us had. We were happy to be reasonable with anyone who was reasonable with us, but Joe would never suffer fools gladly. I remember one gig, I think it was when we supported Be-Bop Deluxe at the Middlesex Poly in December '75, where Joe was at the point of jumping off the stage on to some heckler in the front rows. He ended up pouring a pint of bitter over him, which did succeed in shutting him up. Another gig almost ended up in a brawl with a punter who would insist and insist on hearing Route 66, which we had by then dropped from our set. It's just that the Pistols took their belligerent attitude a step or two further, and by the second time that we played with them, it was more a question of them goading the punter and actually looking for a confrontation.

*

Meanwhile the band carried on with its non stop schedule. The beginning of April saw us finishing off the BBC sessions with Robinson, and among various gigs, another visit to what was becoming almost a home from home - Wandsworth Prison. There's no doubt that our frequent visits to The Nick were a source of inspiration for the next song we started to work on in rehearsals. Also, at this time the "Free George Davis Campaign" was starting to hit the headlines in the media, and Joe drew on both these elements when he wrote the words to "Gaol Guitar Doors". This was a further development in Joe's writing as it was the first song that he wrote with a direct socio-political comment on contemporary affairs.

By now the influence that Dan would have in rehearsals was much stronger. From the inception of the songs he would have a big input in their development - the chord structure, the vocal harmonies and the arrangement in general. Potentially this was great news, but at this time the first hints of the problems to come began to surface. Various factors combined which resulted in a subtle change in the dynamics of the band. There were now, with Clive and Dan, two very capable musicians working together, but there was something in the essential chemistry of the group that had changed, and at the end of the day it was for the worse. Joe was more subdued in the band room; I think he was slightly overawed, although at the time we never talked of it. A distinct polarization developed, with Dan and Clive on one hand, and Joe and myself on the other.

In addition to this there were other negative factors. His close relation with Palmolive was under pressure, and then there was the general success, or lack of it, of the band. On the face of it we were getting somewhere – there was no shortage of gigs, we had just finished the BBC sessions, and we were waiting to sign the Chiswick contract for the single release. But to counter this was the fact that Eddie and the Hot Rods (who might have been considered in some way our most direct "rivals", although truth is I never saw it like that) had just been signed to a major and were now recording an album. Joe was always intensely competitive and I think he probably considered this a slap in the face for us. Things of course had changed considerably from how they had been just a year previously when we were playing our first gigs at The Elgin. We were without doubt an innocent and essentially naïve bunch when we started, but by now the pure joy and novelty of it all for us was starting to wear thin. What were the aims of the band now? What was the point of it all, and where did we see it going?

These questions were thrown up at our next gig down at the Nashville, on the 23rd April, supported again by the Sex Pistols. By now there was no question. Something new was starting to happen. The majority in the Rooms might have come to see us, but the Pistols stole the show and the headlines. Apart from the fact that they sounded great – they'd brought in a good PA and I think it was Dave Goodman on the mixing deck, it was the night of the infamous fight instigated by Goldman or someone from the Pistol's posse. Even at the time it seemed to be a pretty blatant tactic to create a stir in the music press. If that was the ploy, then it worked a treat – the band was fast becoming notorious. Maclaren had everything in place. As a backdrop to it all were various essential factors. Firstly, the gaping hole that many kids felt existed when looking for a shared identity of their own, and secondly, a band that was capable of making it happen on stage. Add to this the capacity of Maclaren for inventing an original "look" and actually being able to produce it and sell it from his shop down in Chelsea. Lastly of course was the managerial savvy he had for manipulating the whole package and of moving it in the media. No need here to spend money on ads in the papers! Whether you liked the Pistols or not, they were big news and even if the group itself didn't grab the music press headlines then the odd staged outrage by their following would and did!

The impressions of the phenomenon second time round were confirmed. For me the band were certainly no slouchers. Steve had a very effective and powerful guitar sound, Paul was a solid no nonsense drummer, Glen was a fine bass player, and Rotten sang with venom in a class of his own. But it was as a unit that they stood out; they were young, totally irreverent and importantly Johnny had developed a very original vocal style. As for their entourage they struck me as they had the first time. Maclaren appeared to me an insufferable snob and brazen manipulator, and the rest of them seemed just too bothered about how they looked for my liking. Add to that the hankering for a gratuitous violence, and it left me pretty cold.

I might not have liked certain aspects of what was happening but its effectiveness just couldn't be denied. This was the future whether you liked it or not, and it screamed at you in the form of a snarl from Johnny Rotten's throat.

High fashion!

Joe of course was more aware of the significance of what was happening than any of us. Apart from our first hand experience, he had always been an assiduous reader of the music papers and the impact that the Pistols were having was enormous. Something new was actually happening, and from the page length reports in the press that followed the gig, and the articles and press interest that was to follow the Pistols from that moment, it was clear that there were going to be big changes ahead.

It's difficult not too overestimate the power and influence of the specialized music press at that time. The weeklies – NME, Sounds, and Melody Maker (all based in London) had huge circulations all over the country, and their influence was far reaching. It was as if all popular music culture was almost shackled to their columns, especially for those bands struggling to get noticed. The 101'ers had already experienced their power. Just a small mention had been enough to get us our first gigs, and the continuing support from Allan Jones and others, had undoubtedly helped in our albeit limited success to date. Maclaren knew how to play the press from the start. The punk explosion just around the corner was to spawn a new generation of journalists, which, particularly at the start of the "movement", formed a close symbiosis with the new bands.

The realization of the beginnings of a new "underground" London scene, had an immediate, if subtle, effect on Joe. His performances became even more intense than they had been, and there crept in an element that had not been there before. Whether it was influenced directly by Rotten's sneer, or was a result of the increasing frustration that he felt, or more probably as a result of both, he became a more bellicose Joe than before. In a way it was almost as if he had something more to prove, not only to the growing number of young punks that would come to the gigs, but also maybe as if the threat to his preponderance during rehearsals had to be more than compensated for by complete dominance when on stage. That was fine by me. Without doubt we performed some of our best gigs in April and May, with Joe absolutely at his wild best.

I remember one gig at the Red Cow in Hammersmith. It was in mid May, and as Clive noted in his diary the crowd that we would now pull would contain, apart from our original fans, a high proportion of young musicians and members of the still fledgling punk community. There would be Pistols, future Clashites and GenerationX's, Bishops, Hot Rods, Stranglers, and God knows how many more kids who within a few months would have formed their own bands. Half way through the set Joe realized his trousers had fallen apart. He didn't bat an eyelid as he winged his way through a chat with the audience while changing his pants up there on the front of the stage.

Another gig we did at this time was two nights in the Roundhouse as support to Bowie's old band – "Spiders from Mars", and Hamill's "Van der Graaf Generator". They were memorable for me for two reasons. The first night Trouble the hound wandered up onto the stage and cool as could be sat down in front of the bass drum to watch and listen to the proceedings. And this during an epic rendition of Gloria at the end of the set! Joe of course latched on to things quickly and called Trouble over to him to scratch his ear. Joe was a brilliant improviser in such circumstances. Nothing would faze him, and he would draw out the positive from what could upset a lesser performer. Hecklers would be the perfect excuse for a quick breather, a banter, and a quick swig on his beer.

The following night Joe and I nearly came to blows on stage. We were in the final throws of the mega ending at the end of Gloria, where literally Joe and I would use up literally every last bit of energy before I would crash out the song and the set. Joe was ready to stop a bar or two before me, and hit one of my cymbals as a sign to "stop now for gawd's sake". I didn't take at all kindly to someone bashing my kit, and leapt up from my drum stool with a fist poised to strike. We looked angrily at each other for a split second, and then realized what the hell, and finished off the song with an even more violent demolition of the kit than usual. But that wasn't the normal tone of our relationship. We got on great, and for me he was tops.

The fact is though that relationships within the group were becoming strained. We only worked on one new song in the next few weeks – "Keep Taking the Tablets": a tune inspired by a quip from the audience at one of our Wandsworth gigs. Again, Dan was heavily involved in its composition, and in fact it was, I think, a very strong pop tune, although along with "Gaol Guitar Doors", we never made it into a studio to record it. We'd call it our psychedelic number because of a strange feed-back Clive would get out of his guitar during the middle eight sections. It did, however, along with "Doors", enter the set list, and by now almost all the set was comprised of original numbers, except for three diehard covers, namely "Gloria", "Junco Partner" and Bo Didley's "Don't Let it Go".

Chapter 9   End of the Road

May followed its course. We signed the deal with Chiswick, agreeing to release the original "Keys to Your Heart" version that Roger had produced at Pathway. The decision to allow them to use as the B side our production of "5*Rock'n'Roll Petrol" (recorded at the BBC with Jeffes and Robinson) was a strange one, and nearly thirty years later I would rue that we had made it. After all, there were fine versions of "Rabies from the Dogs of Love" and "Sweet Revenge"; both from the Pathway sessions that we could have used. We must have felt that the more recently recorded "5 Star" had the edge over them. What green-horns we were. We signed away all our rights to the song for "perpetuity and throughout the world" on the same terms as if it had been a Chiswick produced song. Whatever, a release date was set for mid June, and meanwhile our gig schedule didn't let up.

I was pleased to see that we had landed a gig at the City of London University supporting Geno Washington. He had been the first live act I had ever seen as a fifteen year old, and his album, "Hand Clapping, Foot Stomping, Funky But LIVE" the first LP I had bought. So here I was playing support to him ten years later. It caused him to smile as we chatted in the dressing room about the gig I'd seen.

But smiles were in short supply at Orsett Terrace. The group would function at gigs but there was stagnation in the rehearsal room. The magic had gone, and Joe's was a brooding presence. He had by now virtually split with Paloma and when we didn't have a gig he'd spend more time away from the house, more often than not consuming large quantities of alcohol. We did a particularly hot set down at Camberwell Art School towards the end of the month, and I was surprised at the virulence with which Joe had a go at Clive in the dressing room after the show. He was basically slagging him off for not moving around enough on stage. Joe wanted more action, more intensity from his cohorts, but of course Clive was not one to be bullied in to changing his persona. He had always been the most mild mannered of us all: Mr Steady really, and I think there was no way he could have changed even if he'd wanted to. The end for him was not long in coming. Joe decided on his own, or at least he never talked to me about it, probably because he doubted my supporting him. I have since often wondered why it was Clive rather than Dan that got the axe at this particular point, because I think that the problem really resided in Joe's relation with him rather than with Clive. Possibly the reasons for that were twofold. Firstly, it had been just five months previously that we had invited Dan to take over the bass, unceremoniously dumping Mole out of the band, and to now sack Dan would have been to openly admit the folly of that move. Joe was a proud man, and I don't think would have liked to admit that mistake. Secondly, was the simple necessity of Dan in the creative process of the band at this time. Clive too was of course heavily involved in this process, but not to the extent of Dan who had by now all but taken on the direction of rehearsals – when we did them that is.

The writing was now on the wall, although ever the optimist, I still held out for a solution to the band's problems one way or another. We quickly looked for a replacement for Clive, and found one in the excellent ex Chilli Willi and the Red Hot Peppers, ex Jive Bombers guitarist – Martin Stone, but it was really a stop-gap solution. He of course moved around the stage as little as Clive had done, was more or less the same age, and had a similar kind of image, and these were the very factors that had decided Clive's demise! We were to do just three gigs with him.

My first serious misgiving as to where Joe was at surfaced after a gig in the Golden Lion, Fulham. There were furtive looks and a disappearing act by Joe after the show, and I at last realized something serious was in the air. Of course we were later to discover that it was after this gig that Joe had been given an ultimatum by a certain Bernie Rhodes: 24 hours to dump the 101'ers, or something to that effect. The crunch came a couple of days later. It was around three in the morning and I was fast asleep with Esperanza on our platform bed I had built in our room at Orsett Terrace. Joe climbed the ladder, and shook my shoulder:

- "Snakes .... Are you awake?? I've got something important to tell ya…"

I really knew what it was before he said it. I had shared an intense period of two years with Joe and there had developed a very close, often subliminal, level of communication, although it was true that Joe had been particularly taciturn over the last few weeks. In retrospect, that is easy to explain. Joe was a very loyal person and I think he would have felt a strong sense of guilt merely at the thought of disbanding the group. And it would have been not just with me and the immediate circle involved, but of course with our old and close friends in the squatting community from the early days of the band, not to mention the ever increasing number of new fans. His discontent with the state of things in the group, and his awareness, and increasing involvement on a social level with the burgeoning Punk scene combined to leave him with a relatively simple choice. Joe was well aware that Punk was not a one-off wonder, here today gone tomorrow. He had become a regular attendant at the Pistols gigs in the 100 Club, and he realized that the new sub-culture that we had so often dreamed of was actually taking off before our eyes. The Patti Smith gig at the Roundhouse in mid-May had been for Joe as decisive as The Pistols gigs. He had rushed off to her show, immediately after a gig we had at The Torrington in North London. I couldn't make it, and he was to rave about that gig of Smith's for the following weeks, even incorporating a commentary on it into the long middle section of "Gloria" during which he'd get down to having a talk with the audience.

Well the simple choice that Joe had had to make was now presented to me. He'd met some great young guys. They were forming a new band. They had a manager who "knew all the right people". They needed a singer and a drummer. The singer had decided , "YES". What about the drummer?

Decision time.

- "Not now, Joe. We'll talk about it in the morning."

*

I came downstairs the following morning. Joe was still in bed, so I went to Mickey's room to have a chat with him and find out what he knew about what was going on. He wasn't alone. He ruefully introduced me to a visitor I didn't know. It was Bernie Rhodes, and he immediately put my hackles up because of his attitude, virtually ordering Mickey out of his own room so that we could talk alone, and then strutting around the place as if he owned it. He proceeded to deliver what amounted to a speech on various subjects: the state of British society, the pernicious influence of hippies, the new order as he saw it, the importance of popular music culture and other related topics. He was the kind of person that appeared incapable of holding a two way conversation. The harangue that he delivered was basically an affirmation of a new Punk creed, but to me sounded like a hotchpotch of half baked, pseudo, socio-political blarney. Giving him the benefit of the doubt, I was prepared to accept that at least he was half way to being sincere, but his words fell on very sceptical ears.

Maybe my suspicion of any self-justifying panacea for the individual and/or the world's woes goes back to my childhood. The all-encompassing, all-explaining Roman Catholic moral system had taken a very strong hold on me as a kid, until, during adolescence, I had come to the clear conclusion that it was one of the biggest con-tricks ever perpetrated on mankind. "Creeds" were just not for me and the fervour of a Punk dogma was the last thing I wanted to be part of. It reminds me of a meeting I had been invited to in my first year down in London, probably in 1971. I went with some friends to Westminster hall, where the followers of Guru Maharaji (yet another Indian Guru who was flavour of the month among many young people searching for "definitive answers") had organized an event. Despite the enthusiasm of my friends, the scene turned my stomach. Not only the inner circle of his followers, but the whole hall were prepared to bow down and pay homage to this man, the crowd almost arriving to a point of mass adulation! Looking at the smiling Maharaji, I couldn't help feel that any one worthwhile in his position would simply reject this mindless adoration. The whole idea of a "Guru" was a complete anathema to me. I had not rejected the "articles of faith" of the Catholic Church to now fall in with the doctrines espoused by this charlatan.

Joe & Richard... deep in conversation...

Now with Bernie Rhodes in front of me, I felt the same as I had with the little fat Guru. I couldn't help feeling that this prattler in front of me was either a conman of considerable ability, or an idiot with a head-full of half truths. Either way it made no difference to me. He could not persuade me with any of his theories. Almost from that moment my attitude to any punk "ideology" was one of distrust.

If punk meant anything, to me it came down to a simple postulation:

"Think for yourself, act on the conclusions that you come to, and don't be put off by the powers that be" ...

But there was nothing particularly new in that. Isn't it a fact that this was exactly the unwritten precept that had under pegged any free thinking person from time immemorial through to us squatter/musos who were there and then attempting to create our own world? The point was that Bernie, following in the close footsteps of his former friend Malcom Maclaren, realized that to achieve success on a wide scale a new movement had to be created, in the same way that, say, the 20th Century art movements such as Dadaism and Surrealism had been founded. To create a new movement the dialectic demanded replacement of an old one, and looking around I suppose the remnants of the 60's Hippies were the only young person cultural group that they could find to fill that role! Rather pathetic really, couldn't have chosen a weaker more ineffectual opponent. Besides which I don't think that in 1976 the notion of a Hippy had much meaning for more than a miniscule percentage of young people.

Bernie also put a lot of emphasis on the new music to be created by the new order. R'n'B and R'n'R were dead, and he weighed in with a scathing attack on our band "The 101'ers". If he seriously thought he would persuade me to dump the group for his new project, this was when he blew it. But exactly what was being said here? If the Pistol's music wasn't based on basic R'n'B, with a dose of "Velvets" and 60's British pop, then where did it come from? I doubted that any of the influential new American bands such as the "Dolls" or "Ramones" would have denied the roots of their music. Was there some outer-galactic musical form that I wasn't aware of? Of course there wasn't, so maybe there were other factors that he was referring to. The tempo of the songs perhaps, or maybe intensity of delivery? Who would tell me that The 101'ers lacked in that department? The lyrical content of the songs perhaps? Joe couldn't put a foot wrong here as far as I was concerned. "Rabies", "Sweet Revenge", "Silent Telephone" ... all brilliant, and he'd even gone overtly political with "Gaol Guitar Doors"!!

Maybe we could be criticized for continuing to include the odd cover in our set, but in my book a good song is a good song is a good song... Why should we throw out Gloria or Junco from the set? They worked on stage and we loved playing them, and that for me was enough. So the grounds for slagging us must have been something else ...of course he eventually let slip that famous rock'n'roll concept "Attitude". I didn't take kindly to lectures in that department. I'd done my first gig a week after having started drumming, and Joe for me was the epitome of attitude, just being himself up on stage week after week. Now, if by changing "attitude" what was really meant was trying to appear tougher than you really were then I wasn't interested. If Bernie had come out straight and said something like "Look, your image sucks, you've got to sharpen things up" then just maybe I'd have given him a second listening. But no, his spiel was a dubiously argued political doctrine, laced with irrelevant snippets of Situationist theory. It really was ironic. a wide ranging lecture on political theory, but we at least had actually been squatting for over two years with all the little hassles involved; one of the few direct practical political actions that you could be involved in.

I'd had enough. I couldn't stand the guy. It was a one way conversation going nowhere. He'd pinched Joe from under my nose, and now he had the cheek to walk in to our house all cocky and sure of himself, thinking the drummer was his for the taking as well. Fuck him. Over my dead body I decided there and then. I stormed out of the room, past a shrugging Mickey in the hall, and out of the front door. I can't remember exactly where I went, but I spent a couple of hours just wandering ... and wondering...

I was pretty sure that there would be no turning back as far as Joe was concerned. It just wasn't in his character. Once he'd decided for himself and announced it to me, then that was that. I'd also gleaned enough from my hour with Bernie to realize that what they were setting up was serious business. Looking at it cool-headedly they had lots going for them. Bernie had let slip his relation to Maclaren and brayed of the burgeoning new "movement", and he was already talking about finding a proper rehearsal studio. I'd worked out who the other musicians were, at least two of them – Mick and Keith, two lads who in the last couple of months had come to a number of our London gigs. Mick had always stood out and I realized he'd fit right in to an image slot with his Keith Richards look, and he seemed an alright bloke.

But the whole thing had hit me like a bomb shell. Of course I knew the precarious state the band was in; how couldn't I, with Clive just ousted and Joe hardly able to talk to Dan, and hankering at the same time to be part of the new scene that was developing. But "The101'ers" for me transcended even these problems and I eventually went back to Orsett Terrace to try and speak to Joe. I imagine Bernie had probably told him something of the "conversation" we'd just had. Joe hardly looked me in the face and sat staring at the floor.

- "We can carry on", was the gist of my tirade. "Bring in the other guys if you want, get rid of Dan if you like, change the name if that's a problem, but no way are we breaking this up to go with that arsehole of a manager".

"It's decided Snakes. He's got to be part of it."

And that was that. The 101'ers were no more.

At least, no more apart from one gig we had booked in a couple of day's time, and we had decided to do. To say I was pissed off is of course an understatement. I felt positively sick as we went down to Sussex in Dave the V.D.'s van on the 5th of June for the last gig. Clive turned up and we played a couple of tunes with him. Some of Joe's "group to be" also travelled down which was pretty bad taste if you ask me! I later regretted being so gentlemanly with them. They were probably chuckling into their shirtsleeves as they watched their soon-to-be front man going through his paces. I know perfectly well that I was the loser here. Firstly, it was curtains on a band that had become the all important thing in my life. Secondly, I was parting with a musician that I absolutely loved to play with and who I knew was very special, and lastly I was losing a close friend. Things would never be the same again between us, and for the next couple of years we would hardly exchange a word. I felt let down by him, and maybe he felt the same about me. In fact, during the next few years, it was Esperanza who maintained the friendship with Joe, and she became almost a kind of "Go-Between" for us.

Of course looking back there had been another option available. That would have been to have carried on with Dan, maintain the name "The 101'ers" and probably to have offered Clive the guitar spot. That scenario literally didn't even come to my mind! The 101'ers without Joe was inconceivable. Such was the power of the man. Dan faded out of the picture over the next couple of weeks. He was to join The Derelicts: the squat rock band from Frestonia way, who eighteen months previously had introduced us to the possibilities of the Elgin pub as a venue. Before forming his band "Martian School Girls", he recorded a disc with Chiswick Records in 1978. Clive would also be connected to "The Derelicts", or rather with half of their remains after the band had split up. Sue and John formed "Prag Vec", while Grogan sister Barbara and the drummer Richard later formed The Passions, who Clive joined on guitar. Mickey stayed around with Joe, and within a week he was carting off the PA to a Bernie arranged destination. At that point I really should have stuck out for my rights. More than half the cost of PA had been already paid back through the sweat of our brows, but Bernie accepted paying off the remainder, and he got away with it. Fact is, such practical details were totally insignificant at the time. I was pretty much in a state of shock. Just walking past what had been the band room, with my kit standing silent, was enough to spark off a whole gamut of emotions: anger (at the top of the list), resentment, sorrow ... But what the hell I'd made my choice and that was that.

People have since asked me if in fact what had happened was that "I'd backed the wrong horse", or in other words, that my motive for not joining the Clash-to-be, was that at the time I thought they wouldn't be successful. Truth is that that question, like the option of carrying on the 101'ers without Joe, didn't even enter into the equation. Mine was really a gut reaction, with heart ruling head.

Career Opportunities was not a consideration. This was Bernie's set-up and I wanted no part of it, even if it meant parting company with Joe.

"...*The 101'ers were no more...*"

Chapter 10   An Interlude

Life must go on, as they say, but before leaving the corpse to rest, just one more post mortem analysis seems pertinent. I am pretty sure in retrospect, and Joe was to later express the same, that the nail in the coffin of the 101'ers had been put in place, if not hammered home, on a cold and drizzly January night, six months previously. In two fundamental ways the sacking of Mole had been a crucial move. Firstly, despite Dan's enormous subsequent input (and in my opinion improvement) to the formal arrangement of the band's music, it upset fatally the balance and working chemistry of the group. OK, Clive hadn't got on well with Mole, and had been the prime mover in replacing him with Dan, but it had resulted in a much more unstable scenario –Joe ending up being unable to get on with Dan! Secondly, the change had represented a subtle shift in favour of "musical ability" over that maligned and amorphous concept "Attitude". With the advent of the Pistols, Joe had realized that we were out of phase – we'd made a move in precisely the wrong direction! What had actually happened was that we had lived our nursery school period a couple of years previously; too soon if you like. If chaotic freshness was to be the flavour of the day, then our moment had been down at the Telegraph in Brixton, or at the Charlie Pig Dog Club, or the early days of the Elgin… Mole had been a basic part of that period.

Life for me in Orsett Terrace had suddenly become a morbid affair. I'd have to put up with the odd encounter with Mick, Paul, Keith or some other member of the Clan, who would drop in sometimes to see Joe. Not that I felt particular animosity towards them, its just that …… the only analogy I can think of is it was rather like having to sit down for a cup of tea with the bloke who has just stolen your lover. As for Joe, he typically had thrown himself body and soul into the new enterprise. He developed almost a new persona over night. Not limited of course to just the mod-look haircut and drainpipes, he was a more aggressive Joe, Mr Punk in the basic meaning of the word! It was the fervour of the newly converted, and of one thing I was certain – Joe was a believer. His was no pretence, and I'm sure that was part of the reason why his new band ultimately scaled the heights that they did.

A punkette 1976

For me there was a void, and I had to replace it with something. The thought of playing music with others didn't appeal at all. Esp and I decided that an extended journey somewhere wouldn't be a bad idea, but there was a problem – we were of course absolutely broke. I pored through the vacancy lists down at the dole office and eventually came up with an interview at the Royal Geographical Society. They were looking for a cleaner and I was offered the job. It had a few good things going for it, primarily it was just a short walk from Orsett Terrace through Hyde Park down towards the Albert Hall. Then things looked up when I was told to do an in-depth clean up of a document store room at the top of the building. It was a fantastic place – full of old charts and maps, manuscripts, diaries and reports spanning the life of the institution. No one bothered me, and I would spend hours leafing through the old papers. I put in loads of overtime, and by the end of July had mustered a small but sufficient amount for our travels.

A friend had invited us to stay with her in Bologna, Italy, so that was to be our first destination, but just before leaving I received an unwelcome going away present. Chiswick Records had just brought out "Keys to Your Heart" and there was a review of it posted in the Melody Maker. If I was half expecting some kind of sympathetic obituary then I was to be disappointed. Caroline Coon had usurped the space to run an interview with Joe, entitled "From Crud to King" or something along those lines. So this was to be our obituary! The massive music press support that Punk was to receive over the next eighteen months had started, and also the tone had been set for interviews and reports with Joe and the Clash camp whenever the subject of The 101'ers was raised. But that belongs to a later part of this tale.

We boxed up our belongings, took them over to a friend's house, and left Orsett Terrace for good, our room being taken over by a certain Mr John "Vicious" Beverley. We hadn't any clear idea of where we were heading, but we certainly knew how to exist on next to nothing. For weeks we lived on little more than bread, wine, cheese and tomatoes. We spent about three months in Italy, travelling down through Sardinia, and ending up in a small village in Southern Sicily. The hospitality of people was unbelievable. We were even offered an ancient two roomed house to stay in, complete with exquisite domed bedroom, walls covered in gaudy images of Santa Lucia, leaky roof and two enormous wine barrels at our disposition. We occupied our evenings playing the local card games for hours with our welcoming neighbours, ate their most amazing homemade pizzas and pasta, but soon realized that this was heading towards premature retirement in the depths of the Sicilian campina at the ripe old age of 24 years!

On our travels I had been carting around a snare drum in its case, with a pair of sticks and brushes. Of course it was absolutely unnecessary to have taken the drum. Any old table top would have done to practice my paradiddles. But I'd brought it probably as a subconscious symbol for me, rather than for any practical reason. A reminder of what I should really be doing; or what I really wanted to be doing.

We decided to make back for London, but via Andalusia, and we took a four day train journey across the underbelly of Europe. We ended up for a week or so in Granada, where just over two years before I'd waved goodbye to Esperanza, convinced that I'd never see her again. Spain was as vibrant as ever. Franco had gone by now, but the back end of his regime was still just about hanging on to life and power. We went to a political rally and concert, organized to protest at the latest gratuitous killings perpetrated by the Guardia Civil. The atmosphere was buzzing among young people in the city. We suddenly found ourselves in the vanguard of a demonstration heading down the main street, and narrowly avoided a pummelling at the heavy hands of the riot police. I couldn't help comparing young people's relation to the political situation there in the immediate post-Franco Spain, with what was happening back in England, and the essentially nihilistic Punk scene that we'd left exploding into existence a few months earlier. The comparisons didn't come down favourably on the side of the London "revolution". Whereas in Spain for many the concerns were of freedom or fascism, life and death, I couldn't help seeing the English scene as little more than an intelligently manipulated exercise in media control attending the pursuit of fame and fortune.

Well, it was time to find out what had been happening back home and we returned to west London in mid-December.

Chapter 11   Cinderella Transformations

There was certainly a lot of catching up to do, but first we had to find somewhere to live. Big John put us on to a squatted house in Monmouth Road, a cul-de-sac off Westbourne Grove. It was just five minutes from Orsett Terrace, which had been abandoned by its final occupants a couple of months previously, and we were glad to find somewhere in our west London neighbourhood. We shared a flat for a time and then had a stroke of luck. A basement flat at number 27 of the same street became vacant. We went to see the housing association that was managing it, but no, they didn't want it to be used and wouldn't accept our offer of rent. Fine we thought, and occupied it the following day. Two weeks later they contacted us to make it a formal arrangement. It was a large independent flat with a garden out the back, but even so there wasn't really space to hold a rehearsal room. I was itching to get back to playing and soon found a house over in Latimer Road where, despite my noise, Mick and Annie didn't mind me occupying a spare room. Most days I'd go over there to practise and was soon back in to the swing of things.

I thought that after two years of playing it was time for me to look for my first professional teacher, as literally I had learned to play sitting on the stool behind a functioning rock band. Apart from the suggestions and advice of my fellow band members, and a close attention to my record collection, I'd had no formal teaching or even advice from fellow drummers. So now the time was right and I contacted a teacher based in Marylebone. Over the next couple of months he tried to straighten out the horrible habits I'd fallen in to, and basically impressed on me the maxim that I had already arrived at – relax! I'd never had so much time for myself to practise, and I made the most of it, knowing that I'd soon be back in a band where my own time would be in short supply.

The music that I was listening to hadn't changed much from the 101'ers days though, if possible, there was even less straight rock.

Jazz and jazz drummers were still my favourites, despite the incredible things they could do seeming light years from my reach. Seeing Roland Kirk and later Art Blakey in Ronnie Scott's around this time did much to bolster my interest, and it was from the jazz racks that most of my records were bought. Of contemporary music other than jazz, reggae was without doubt the most frequent on my turntable, especially from the likes of Big Youth, King Tubby or Gregory Isaacs, who we saw in a memorable concert later that year. Another big influence was soon to come in the form of Fela Kuti's afro-beat, to which I was introduced by our friend Tom, who was wheeling and dealing in Nigeria and had got to know the music first hand. It combined so many elements that I loved. The funkiest rhythm section that you could imagine, a tight papping horn section, the soulful African women backing vocals, all led by Fela's sax and organ base. Miles away from the music that I would be actually playing, but it was from this kind of music that I would take my cues when practising.

And in early 1977, what of the Punk explosion? Had the fabric of Young London been seduced yet by the New Order? Not really, these were still early days, but big changes were just around the corner. The Pistols had already released their first "Anarchy" single, and on a major label. Other bands, The Damned and Vibrators, also had records out, and the space given to Punk in the record press was enormous; still far out of proportion to the actual level of punter participation at live gigs. Palmolive, who had dived headlong in to the Punk scene, had filled us in with the general news – the Punk festival, the Pistols' Grundy interview, the debacle of the Anarchy tour, the rumours of a big Clash record deal in the offing.... It all left me cold.

Joe came around to see us one night, probably in early March. He really did seem a different man. Not just how he looked, but something much deeper. Gone the ready smile and chuckle. He was so serious, and I remember thinking "Gawd, he's quoting from a rule book!" everything he said appearing to come from a bank of slogans. He mentioned that they were still looking for a drummer and also that they would shortly be playing a London date. This turned out to be at the Harlesden Coliseum, and up we went to see them. There was a large crowd and an air of high expectancy. I think it was The Slits' first gig, and to describe them as shambolic is an understatement, but they were certainly something special. Ariup ranted and raved and all but pulled her hair out to the cavorting beat of Palmolive's drums and the screeching guitar. I remember it seeming a very long night, and when the Clash finally came on, I was of course extremely interested to see for the first time the new band of my old friend. I had to admit they were potent and generated enormous power, but I was struggling with all kinds of feelings – envy, nostalgia, hate, disdain. At the end of the night, I trudged home in a confused state. I could criticise as much as I liked, but at the end of the day there they were on the stage doing it, and doing it pretty damn well. What the hell was I doing?

I started looking around, as it was obvious that it was high time I was playing in a band again. In Monmouth Rd, one of the other squats was occupied by Gina Birch, and I went along to hear a new band she was getting together with Ana da Silva. The Raincoats, as they were called, were fresh and exciting, and were representative of what for me was the one positive thing to come out of the Punk phenomenon – Do It Yourself. Suddenly new bands were appearing like flies in a fish market. Proof was found in a poky, uninviting basement down in Covent Garden. The Roxy was interesting for about half an hour. Just about everyone down there was in a band, or on the point of forming one, but I must say it appeared all very self conscious to me. People seemed as if they were desperately trying to be different, yet would end up seeming all the same. Then there was all that gobbing…. Mind you, I preferred the scene down there in comparison to what I wandered in to one night at the Hope and Anchor in Islington. An unknown band to me, "Dire Straits" were going through their set…

*

Suddenly, just what I was looking for appeared in the form of an old mate - Tymon Dogg. In Chapter 4 I've already outlined his story and the link he'd had first with Joe and then with the 101'ers. Since last playing with him at the Elgin, eighteen months previously, we hadn't had much contact.

Tymon & Richard, 1977

He had finished recording an album Outlaw 1, appropriately named of course, because for me he was most definitely the Number One outlaw. The disc had been recorded for his own label, in his front room, using his innumerable instruments. The first (and only?) truly Punk folk record, because Tymon's music could most definitely be categorized in the "folk" bracket – the violin being his principle instrument, along with an acoustic guitar. And Punk? Well that of course would depend on your definition of Punk.

The name Outlaw Records was appropriate for another reason. The money needed for recording and pressing the album was obtained from a London Transport Police pay off! A few months earlier, Tymon had been stopped while busking down the tube, and had been subsequently assaulted by the police officer. The testimony of various witnesses persuaded London Transport to come to an out of court settlement; enough to finance the album!

If anyone was "his own man" then that person for me was Tymon. The fiercest independence I'd ever encountered in a musician or anywhere else for that matter. If Punk meant anything real, anything other than a piece of clothing, a haircut and studied words, then for me Tymon embodied it. We bumped in to each other one day at 23 Chipenham Road and decided there and then to start a band. Neither his abode nor my practise room were suitable for rehearsing so we set about looking for a space. We got in to a church at the end of Monmouth Road, and Tymon spent a couple of nights in there, but he had to leave – unknown to us, it had been recently bought, and he would have had to share it with the Jehovah's Witness. Then he found a basement to squat in the Great West Road, just a few yards from That Tea Room. A broken placard with the suggestive name "Cinderella Transformations" was hanging from a ground floor window, and Tymon moved in to live in the back room, while we installed the band room at the front, by now considerable expertise having been gained in the sound-proofing department.

It was a treat to be playing with Tymon. He was such a passionate performer, and I'd always loved his songs. And then his whole attitude was so in sync with how I felt. He was the ultimate anti-fashion man, and I suppose we almost revelled in taking a totally independent stance from all that was happening around us. We even went to the extent of calling the band "Tymon Dogg & The Fools". The Fools because we knew that in terms of landing a fat record company advance we just weren't playing our cards right. It was at a time when the A & R men were falling over each other trying to sign bands, and almost all you needed to find a deal was a short haircut, a curling upper lip, a loud electric guitar, and a manic tempo beat.

The kind of music we would play also fitted in with what I wanted at the time. Flat out volume controls on guitar amps had always had a limited attraction for me, and the fact that we were using electrified violin and acoustic guitar lent a jazzier feel to things. There was also such a variety in Tymon's songs that it demanded an appropriate and imaginative response on the part of the drummer. I was to learn a lot with Tymon. Another link that we had was a mutual interest in what was then called International Folk music, now of course - World Music. Back in the mid 70's this was a very minority interest, and just about the only place I remember where you could find recordings was Collets down the Charing Cross Road. I was to become hypnotized first by Bulgarian music, quickly followed by recordings from just about every corner of the globe. Afghanistan, Burundi, Haiti, or China – it didn't matter from where; and often the more obscure looking the record, the greater interest I would have in it. This also led me into the racks of relatively obscure blues and American folk music. Labels such as Arhoolie and Folkways, with gems such as George "Bongo Joe" Coleman, or Texan Penitentiary chain gang recordings, became the favourites on my turntable.

As for the group, we decided that a Trio would be the ideal format for the band, keeping things simple and allowing space with an uncluttered, basically acoustic sound. We went through scores of auditions. Bass player after bass player trouped through the basement, and time after time either they didn't want us or we didn't want them. In fact Tymon and I were fools to have hung around so long looking for the elusive third member. We should have just gone out and done it as a duo, but for some reason we didn't. A couple of times we would end up working with someone for a few weeks before they left or we got rid of them. We started to wonder if the name we'd chosen was having some kind of occult effect, such a high proportion of candidates were distinctly off their rocker! After some months we finally found our man – Ron, and we were ready for our first gig which we did with our friends the Raincoats, down the road at The Tabernacle in Powis Square, an old synagogue converted to community-centre.

Truth is I think that that few people seemed to take our music seriously, but one of the few fans that we did have was Palmolive. The Slits agreed to do a gig with us supporting them, so I set about looking for a venue and came up with a previously unused one, the crypt of Trinity Church in Bishop's Bridge Rd, just around the corner from Orsett Terrace. It was all very basic, there was no bar, no security, nothing except an empty crypt with electricity. We cobbled together a stage, got a friend in to do the PA and string up a few lights, and at the last minute, thank goodness, I called an East End hard-man friend and his mate, both big, potentially mean and with long-time bouncer experience. The Slits were by then, it must have been late '77, making a noise for themselves. They had done the White Riot Tour and had just recorded a John Peel session. They called John Peel to put the news out on his programme and we waited to see whether we'd get enough people in to cover expenses.

It was to be an eventful day in other ways. The night before, Ron had left our rehearsal and made his way back to his squat which was down the West End. Ron was an assiduous "skip-picker", a pastime that could sometimes have relatively rich pickings; especially in his upmarket end of town. It was a completely harmless activity, involving the scouring of builders' waste skips that were parked in the street. Of course down the West End all kinds of stuff could be found in them – I don't have to look further than the fine Victorian chest of draws staring me in the face right now! Picked off the pavement of a Bayswater road thirty years ago by Esperanza, another keen skip-scouring fanatic.

Ron was a very handy man. A fine cabinet maker, always building some musical instrument or other, he would have been particularly interested in finding quality timber – oak panelling or that sort of thing, thrown out during the conversion of someone's flat. In fact, you could say Ron was a fundamental part of the ecosystem; like a maggot's role in the perpetual cycle of death and rebirth.... Anyway, some bored policemen had spotted him going about his business, challenged him, and then charged him ostensibly on suspicious behaviour and "intent" to commit a felony; in reality because they didn't like his demeanour, and he had probably told them to mind their own business. All this resulted in him being carted off to West End Central police station and subsequently down to Brixton prison.

The first we heard of it was a call I received at two o'clock on the day of the gig from the probation officer at the nick. This was serious news. If I remember things right, I first had to find someone with money to stand bail, and then shoot off to West End central and then to Brixton prison. The probation officer was a decent fellow. He had taken to heart Ron's insistence that there was to be an all important event later that night, had taken the trouble to track me down, and then at Brixton had helped us through the red tape. He even turned up at the gig later that night, more, I imagine, out of curiosity than out of professional obligation.

Ron and I finally made it to the venue in the nick of time, and what a sight met our eyes. The John Peel plug had worked beyond all expectation. It was as if all London Punkdom had decided to come down to the gig, and suddenly we had over five hundred people crammed in to the crypt. I cast an inquisitive glance at big-hearted Bob the Bouncer:

"Nuffin' to worry 'bout Rich. Everyfin' under control." tapping what I imagined to be the wad of takings in his inside jacket pocket. "Nice bunch of friends you got 'ere …."

cocking a thumb at the black - clad hordes crammed in to every corner of the murky crypt.

We'd arrived with no time for a sound check - just plug in and take it away. Making the most of our position as "promoters" of the gig, we played through a full set of Tymon's songs: getting on for an hour and a half. Maybe too much for some of the punters. Imagine the crowd we had pulled in. Almost all dyed-in-the-wool Punk freaks weaned on a diet of NME and very loud and fast rock with safety pins. It must have all seemed rather incongruous to many. The "Hippy-Hating" line that had been started by Maclaren and then taken up by the Clash & Co was still very much in the air. The "You're either with us, or against us" discourse was a potent means in helping create the New Order, but in fact it was a classic political propaganda tactic, and it resulted in polarizing positions and a fascist dismissal of other ways of thinking, or (especially at this facile stage in the proceedings) of dressing.

Tymon Dogg & The Fools...Richard, Tymon & Ron

Ours was very much an anti-image. Tymon had cut his hair short on one side of his head, leaving it longish on the other, and it was balanced in reverse order, by a moustache on one side of his lip, but not on the other. An exercise in anarchic asymmetrical hair cutting, you might say. I was sporting a goatee at this time, and my ubiquitous hat, and we didn't call Ron "The Tassel" for nothing. You might think I'm being oversensitive on this point. Did appearance really have such importance at this time? Well, yes unfortunately to so many people I think it did!

And what of the music? We went down surprisingly well. The passion in Tymon's performances could never be denied, and despite the unorthodox line up including, on some numbers, Ron's home made two string bass for bowing, and Tymon's harmonium operated by that furiously pumping leg, the crowd was in general appreciative. I don't know if the PA was up to delivering the vocals in any decipherable form, but if it had been the public would have been treated to the acid wit and incisive commentary of Tymon's lyrics.

Finally, the stage was set and The Slits came on. Always for me one of the most enjoyable Punk bands, their freshness was endearing and mesmerizing, and at that time they were at their best, the music much more together than at the Coliseum, yet still retaining the innocence which was at the heart of their appeal. They of course brought the house down, and nearly the PA as well. By now the crypt was completely packed – there just wasn't room to move. To get a better view someone jumped up on to the table supporting the mixing desk. The table collapsed, and I remember having to actually hold up the mixing desk for a good few minutes, while the sound engineer carried on with his job and someone went off to look for a replacement table.

We'd made a good few bob on the door, which hadn't been the reason for setting up the gig, but was of course a very welcome bonus. As for The Fools, we received hardly a mention in the music press, and what did appear was predictably depreciatory. What might have been a help for us in terms of exposure and the search for gigs didn't happen. We slogged on, recorded some material on an eight track, but gigs remained hard to come by. Looking back it was great working on the songs, and it was always fun working with Tymon, but as time went by there was an underlying feeling of frustration with what we were doing, or rather with the lack of response to it. Still, we really were just reaping what we had sown. We hadn't called ourselves The Fool's for nothing, and from the beginning we knew we were up against it. Its just that you have to live with the hope that things are going to turn out. Sometimes they do, and sometimes they don't, and this time things just weren't happening for us.

*

This feeling of frustration came to the fore one night in early May. The Clash's White Riot tour which had taken them around the country came to an end at the Rainbow. It really was the "coming of age party" for the band. With two or three thousand people packed in to the North London venue, they could rightly feel that they'd "made it", and Joe would cite it later as one of the high points in the Clash story. Well, for my story it perhaps represented a corresponding low point! I hung around at home, broodingly downing a few whiskies whilst deciding whether to go or not. Eventually I made my way up there, or should I say staggered, and somehow managed to blag my way backstage, literally minutes before they were due to start. I was having a few words with Joe, when suddenly from behind me I hear:

"Who's that fucking arsehole in the hat, then?"

It was pretty obvious that the derogatory remark was directed at yours truly – being the only one present wearing a hat and probably some other equally "uncool" clothing, this being a time of de rigueur leather pants, plastic bag dresses and razor blades. I turned round to discover the source of the insult and replied to the scowling Pistols' guitarist Steve Jones. With a:

"What's your problem you fuck face bastard wanker…"

… or something along those lines, and I took a drunken lunge at him. We ended up rolling on the floor, with me almost certainly getting the worst of things. The fracas ended with some bouncer unceremoniously dragging me out of the dressing room. It was probably the last thing Joe would have wanted to deal with, seconds before taking the stage, as he came out and checked to see what the damage was!!

There were some interesting little coincidences in the event. Steve was probably as envious as me of the Clash's success, the Pistols (because of their notoriety) having few chances to gig at that time. Basically behind it all was the fact that both him and I wanted to be up there under the lights! And there was a rather comic symbolism in me having a go at a member of the band which, a year previously, had been one of the main reasons for my previous band's demise.

In the days following, however, I felt as if I still had a score to settle with Steve! My job at the time needs a small introduction. I had become the driver of a Selfridges Store delivery van. In fact the chore had good things going for it. My mate and I shared the same attitude in that we both wanted nothing more than to get things over as quickly as possible. We were invariably the first ones out of the depot by half eight in the morning, and I became an adept negotiator of west London traffic – our green Bedford van tearing around our patch, which would include an area stretching from Notting Hill, through Hammersmith and sometimes out to the Surrey commuter belt. Our lively attitude would usually result in us being back home by midday, although I wouldn't take the van back till late in the afternoon, and we would get paid for a full day's work. It also resulted in me having a vehicle for carting things around, which would of course came in useful when I had to move my drums or PA equipment.

I remember the next few days after the Rainbow brawl, scouring the streets of London with my black eye on the look out for Steve, ready to leap out and finish our business.

Chapter 12   Getting Around

My liaison with Tymon finally ended, at least for the time being, in early '78. Two reasons really. Firstly Ron was going through a rough patch, and I couldn't face the thought of auditioning yet more bass players, and secondly, the frustration of not getting anywhere quicker got the better of me. I had run out of patience, and with so much going on around me musically, felt it was time to move on. For me it felt like only a temporary suspension of our collaboration, and so it turned out to be, as we were to cross paths at various times in the future, but The Fools were finished – you could even say we had truly lived up to our name!

For a few gigs I worked with "The Raincoats" while they looked for a permanent replacement for their recently departed drummer. No violin yet, and apart from Ana's guitar and Gina's bass they were playing with Jeremie, an American girl lead guitar player, who's guitar hero antics didn't really suit the direction in which Ana and Gina were heading. One gig we did at the Marquee, supporting the punk band "Chelsea", I remember for one overriding reason – the continual shower of gob and spittle that spewed from the throats of our pathetic audience, landing like a snow blizzard on the stage and of course on us. I got in to a tangle with some idiot punter who had sent in his spittle as accurately as a blitzkrieg bomb aimer, and who landed just one too many masses of phlegm on the person of this captive drummer. This particular punter participation fad seemed to sum up the state things had got to in punk by early/mid '78. Mindlessness was the name of the game. I had no sympathy, in fact more like downright contempt, for the average Joe Bloggs at the gigs. At least at the start of the Punk Explosion, there had been a strong element of individuality and self-expression.

The Raicoats in The Marquee 1977...Ana, Gina, Jeremie & Richard

This, inevitably you might think, was quickly degenerating in to just another fad. The Weekend Punk would don his fancy dress, come up to one of the West End clubs such as the awful Vortex, see one band after another invariably playing by now what sounded like formula music, and if the latest craze was to spit at the group – well, that's what you did...

I was looking around to start a new band and out of the blue, or rather the drizzle of Bell Street market, I met Dewart, an enigmatic ivory tinkler with a bunch of good tunes under his arm and dark shadow on his brow. The balance of things was restored when I met Dave Scott, a nifty guitar player who didn't need much encouragement to try out his vocal chords. Dave was a bubbly, creative character whose first love had been painting. He had gained certain local notoriety by the inclusion of an explicit masturbation scene on one of the canvases in his latest exhibition, which had severely upset one of the local town councillors.

139

We set up rehearsals in the basement of Dave's house near King's Cross. The name we eventually settled on for the group was "Bank of Dresden". No real meaning to it; I suppose we liked the sound of it, and the vague and improbable image that it might suggest. The quartet was completed with the recruitment of Jane Crockford on the bass. She had hardly played before but was very quick to learn, and within a few weeks we had a set sorted. Most of the songs were originals, the only covers that I can remember being a Bo Didley number called "I'm Goin' Home" that I would sing, and a version "Mac The Knife" done with a ska/reggae feel to it. For the rest, Dave and Dewart between them came up with ideas for songs that we would knock about at rehearsals. The music was a strange concoction. I can't even remember the keyboard Dewart used. Was it a Rhodes? Whatever, Dave quickly become an effective frontman, Jane was great on bass, and I made sure we rocked.... For our first gig I found an upstairs room in a pub on Westbourne Park Road, "The British Oak". It was the first time that they had allowed a rock band in there, and I think the last after our raucous affair. For the gig we made contact with a sax player, John Glyn, who agreed to do the gig after a quick rehearsal. He'd done stuff for Wreckless Eric, and had previously been with X-Ray Spex, and apart from being a great blower he was a good bloke to have around, and he became a semi-permanent fixture in the band, depending on his other commitments.

There followed a pretty uneven six months. The highs were the gigs, when we managed to find them. One of the early ones that I particularly remember was at the Africa Centre in Covent Garden. We had to hire the place and promote the gig ourselves. Through a mutual friend of their singer I got in an unknown band "The Psychedelic Furs" as our support, along with neighbour Neal Brown's Tesco Bombers. The publicity worked and we packed the place, but most of the time venues were hard to find, and we ended up looking for someone to help out on the managerial side of things. We also booked ourselves into an eight track studio somewhere in east London, where we recorded four demo tracks.

Dave & Richard in the Bank of Dresden

It was the old story really. The initial Punk boom was coming to an end and the music scene in London, despite its rejuvenation, was settling down to its old pattern. The major record companies hadn't taken long in realizing that they would have to jump on board, or be left behind. Despite the success of the likes of Mute, Stiff etc, the majors were right back in the driving seat, and although there were more opportunities for new bands than in the run up to '76, it was of course back to the same procedures as of old if you wanted to land a deal. Your demo tape cassette would join the piles already scattered over the desk of the A&R manager's secretary: "He's too busy to see you right now. Just leave it with me and we'll call you back next week...." Contacts with journalists for the all important write-up of your gig were a must, and there was always the sneaking feeling that the image portrayed in some decent photos of the band could be almost more important than the music you were making! And this just so that someone from the company office might bother to make it down to your next gig!

Not long after the introduction of the manager (in fact an old acquaintance of mine), the unity of the band began to flounder. Inevitably, I suppose, it was on the rocks of "interfering management" that the group disintegrated. Why is it that managers always assume they know all the answers; up to the point even of changing the chords of that chorus, making the words more accessible, adding a sax solo here, a rhythm guitar there ..... never mind questions of image and dress! After some internal skulduggery, we decided to call it a day, Dave later joining Spizzenergi, while Jane became a founder member of all girls group The Modettes.

*

The absence of having a regular band did have its advantages for me. There really was a frenetic musical activity in London at the time. Bands, or perhaps more accurately Projects, would surface, evaporate, and later reappear often having undergone some strange mutation. One such scheme was a big band set-up that I organized with a fine trombone player, whose name escapes me, but to who I was introduced by a friend. In the sessions we had two drum kits – myself and Nick, percussion, bass a couple of guitars, 3 or 4 saxes including John Glyn and Inigo, the trombonist and a trumpeter friend of his. The music was pretty loosely based I suppose on a Fela type line up, in a Miles's "Witches' Brew" period style, although in terms of accomplishment I shudder to even mention these names with us in the same breath! I remember some heavy ska-like rhythms with honking long-chord horn section riffs. Good fun to play; if only I could find the tape we recorded on an old Revox I'd acquired.

Another interesting set up was organized by a neighbour of ours. Neal Brown's dead-pan lyrics and tongue-in-cheek pop found expression in his "Vincent Units"; a group that also morphed in to "The Tesco Bombers". Apart from the previously mentioned Nick and Inigo, trumpeter Richard Summer and percussionist/drummer Derek Goddard were also irregular members of the outfit, and they both became close friends with who I would play with in later formations.

Other collaborations would be even more sporadic. One evening I got a call from a friend of a friend whose band had suddenly lost their drummer to the long reach of the law, and it had to be on the afternoon of their first and long awaited gig at Dingwalls. I had never heard their music before, and the only time for rehearsal was a couple of songs at the sound check. Shock horror when I discover "The Balloons" were in to some kind of beefheartian, a-rhythmic, but highly structured progressive rock. An absolute nightmare of a gig for an unrehearsed drummer, as any sense of a regular beat would suddenly fall from beneath you, just as you felt you had it!

Meanwhile, life was a carefree affair. We didn't need much money to exist, and I always managed to find some part time work to hold things together. At the same time I was able to play music with the people I wanted, even though there would be invariably no money in it. You could almost say it became an unwritten rule for me, but in fact it was a thing beyond conscious decision. Either I got on with and liked the people with whom I was playing, or I would find it impossible to work with them. For me and I think most people, playing music in a small group format is such an intense business that you can almost compare it to a love affair.

Talking of which, I was still involved with Esperanza. She had continued taking evening classes in art and had been accepted on to a degree course at Camberwell Art School. She was so involved in her work, now concentrating on ceramics, that I think it had much to do with the fact that our relationship survived the ups and downs of our pretty crazy life style.

Vivian the bag lady on Westbourne Grove

It was a question of "live and let live" for both of us, but at the end of the day we were lucky to able to retain both the passion and the mutual respect necessary for our relationship to endure.

Our basement flat in Monmouth Road, just off Westbourne Grove, became a bit of a hang out for many people. The fact that we never had a TV perhaps had something to do with it, but there would be a progression of people calling in for a spliff, a cup of tea and a natter. Even Vivian, the half crazed bag lady from the Grove would sometimes knock on our door for a cuppa. Poor thing, you would usually find her huddled on a broken cardboard box on the pavement outside the 24 hours super. Surrounded by her possessions - a pile of plastic bags, her clothes would be half hanging off her; she'd be filthy and nattering away to her personal devils. In reply to your: "Hello Vivian, everything alright?", her face would suddenly light up in an intelligent smile, as she'd ask after the health of the Mrs. We had offered her the use of our garden tool shed if the street were to ever get too cold and wet for her, but no - she went her own way...

Another regular visitor was Keith, the old Australian sea captain who had lived above That Tea Room. He was a regular for supper, and given the sparkle of his tales, we were more than happy indulge him and his wild imagination!

One morning Esperanza noticed a huddle lying in the garden at the back of the house. Was it Vivian? No. What a surprise when we find it was Joe. He'd arrived in the early hours, found the flat in darkness, and rather than waken us, decided to sleep among the plant pots and garden tools. We greeted each other with a wary grimace. Though the ice was slowly thawing, for me there was still the shadow of betrayal, and I accusingly asked him if he'd heard the cock crow yet, in a rather oblique reference to the three times denial by St. Peter. He had recently suggested in some interview that the name "The 101'ers" had been given to the band because of the number on the torture cell in Orwell's "1984". There was a fair slice of irony in that comment! One of Orwell's prime observations in the book had been the use by fascist governments of "Doublespeak" the deliberate distortion of truth. Here was Joe denying what in fact was a genuine piece of "political" reality: squatting, to distance himself from a "hippy" past, and replace it with a concept that sounded good within the Bernie Punk Political Panorama.

I always felt that in the first year or so after the Clash's inception, Joe was put on, or rather put himself on, a fierce psychological rack. It was as if the only way he could go through with his new role was to take it to its most extreme, denying at the same time all that his recent past had been. Certainly most of what he declaimed in public at this time I think should be taken with a pinch of salt! He created, and I think totally believed in, this other Punk Persona: a tough guy with more than a fleck of arrogance, which better accorded with his present role. "From Crud to King" as he had proclaimed to Coon in the M.M. In fact we knew another Joe - carefree and kind with that impish grin, always with time for other people and their well-being, and I knew which of the two Joes I preferred.

It reminds me of an event that had happened a couple of years previously in the early days of the 101'ers. One freezing January night in 1975, Esperanza and I were sitting with some friends in the kitchen of our squat in 101. We were probably attempting to keep warm from the burners of the gas stove as we sipped our tea from the jam jar tea cups.... Who should stumble through the door but Joe, soaked to the skin, water creating puddles on the floor, his hair plastered to his skull, teeth chattering as he attempted to tell us what had happened. As we bundled him up to his room looking for towels and blankets, the story emerged. He'd been walking back home up the Great West Road, just past Westbourne Park Road tube station where the humped bridge straddles the Grand Union Canal next to That Tea Room.... He'd heard a splash and a shout, had rushed along the bank, and seen a shadowy figure thrashing his arms in the murky water. Off with his beaten up old leather jacket, Joe had jumped in after the fellow, dragged him to the bank, and hauled him out. Just a drunk, tired of life, thinking to drown his sorrows and a bit more ..... Woody, as he was still known at that time, played down the whole event, and didn't catch pneumonia, which was just as well as we'd have had a gig down the Charlie Pig Dog Club a few days later...

A lot had changed in the intervening years. Not least Joe had achieved the fame he had always hankered after. For the first time since our band had ended we sat in the basement, had a cuppa and a chat; even had a laugh reminiscing over the good times we'd shared.

*

Many a rave up was held down in that basement. We'd need little excuse to roll up the carpets and throw open our doors.

Esperanza & Richard, Monmouth Road, 1978

It would soon become packed with a hotchpotch of people from West London and beyond, the night invariably ending at the local bakery with the first light of dawn. And if it wasn't at our place then there would be a party somewhere or other. One affair that stands out in my mind took place in a huge squatted mansion in I think Russell Square in Bloomsbury. We arrived as the resident band "The Homosexuals" were starting their set. What a crazy scene. The group was something else. Deconstructed power-pop with irreverence for just about every norm in the book. This for me was punk in its truest sense It was the first time I met Jim the Bass, who was to become a close friend and musical cohort, but more of him later. One spring afternoon in '79 I received a phone call that resulted in me quickly boxing up my drums and driving off to a flashy recording studio in Shepherds Bush.

Chapter 13   No Birds do Sing

I wasn't sure what to expect as I was directed down a corridor in Virgin's Townhouse studio complex. The call had been from Keith Levene, guitarist of Public Image Limited (PiL), and he had been very emphatic:
- "Come down straight away, bring your drums if you want, but we have a kit here anyway…"

I knew Keith from the last days of The101'ers, as a punter at gigs or when he'd occasionally come around to Orsett Terrace. He had been one of the founder members of The Clash, and although I had never crossed more than a couple of words with him, there was something I had liked about his mercurial presence, as you might catch just a glimpse of a shock of blond hair as it flashed through a door. He introduced me to John and Wobble. The last time I had talked to John had been at the infamous Nashville gig three years previously when the fledgling Pistols had supported The 101'ers. Wobble I didn't know, but we didn't waste any time. I went over to the large drum booth to check out the kit. It was fine, and was miked-up, so I just had to adjust a few things and within next to no time we were laying down some tracks.

I was impressed with their recording method. Wobble would start a riff that I would latch on to, or I would be tinkering around with a drum pattern for which Wob would start playing a bass line. Meanwhile Keith and John would be in the control booth from where we would hear a shout of "go for that, we're recording", or Keith might suggest another approach, or the tape machine would just be left on record…   Eighteen hours later, and I crawled out of the studio in the early hours of the morning to a painful shock. My car had been forced and my Pearl kit had been nicked. What an idiot. I'd left the drum kit in full view on the back seat of my beaten up old Morris Oxford. Still, it had been a productive night's work, and we had a couple of rhythm tracks down: one being a track that we recorded with a heavy emphasis on the toms, and incidentally, with the tom tom thumping style of my sister-in-law Palmolive very much in mind. The guitar for the song was later worked on by Keith, and John then wrote some fine words for what was to become "No Birds Do Sing".

Despite the loss of my kit I was very excited with the new development. I got on with the three of them fine, and over the next couple of weeks we recorded and part-mixed a number of tunes. "Memories", "Socialist", a version of "Death Disco", and my favourite "Chant" were all laid down, apart from a number of other rhythm tracks that I haven't heard of since. The method was the same for all of them. Put down the rhythm track, and later layer-in guitars, synth, and voice. Simple and very effective. The influence of dub reggae's earth shuddering bass sound was not lost on Wobble. He was the kind of bass player I liked to play with, keeping things simple, but at the same time coming up with great bass lines.

There was also no prejudice in terms of musical styles. My favourite pop had always been soul and funk based, so what a pleasure it was to be in a happening band that absolutely loved reggae and black music in general, and weren't afraid to espouse the Disco beat - hated by any true Punk rocker at the time! They were up for anything based on a driving rhythm which suited me fine. Keith had a very quick musical brain. He was the kind of guitar player that would always look for something different. Same on the mixing desk - full of ideas, very creative and willing to try anything out.

John was of course the quiet boss of the set-up. A great singer, he could write spot on lyrics, and the more I got to know him the more I liked him – this, the odious bête-noire of late 70's British society. As you've probably gathered, I had never been the greatest fan of the "Pistols Phenomenon", primarily down to the ever-present hand of their manager moving the pieces; and on coming in to the Pil camp, despite the publicized standoff that John and Maclaren were engaged in, I was a little dubious as to the present motives of John, and certainly intrigued as to what was beneath his Public Image. Over the following weeks the doubts were to quickly recede. I came to realize he had a genuine love of music and an interest in doing something original with it. I also found that, in terms of the music biz, the ethos behind Pil was the same as mine.

I discovered, for example, that my disdain for the "Bernie Punk Clash Creation" was wholly shared by my new outfit. I suppose that both Keith and myself would have shared a particular dislike for Bernie given our experiences at the start of the Clash, but there was certainly more to it than that. The Pil ideal was most definitely rooted in the "Do It Yourself" philosophy, and at the start of my involvement with them I suppose you could say it was like a dream come true for me, sharing with them scorn for the blind followers of fashion that London was crawling with at the time...

John was intent on resurrecting Lydon from Rotten, and good on him I thought. Having had his fill of Malcolm's machinations, he had quite simply set up an organization free from a manager's interference. An old friend of his, Dave Crowe, who also lived at the house in Gunter Grove, looked after general paper work – accounting, printing etc, while Keith's then girl friend, Jeannette, would help out liaising with the Virgin office and other bits and pieces. Meanwhile there was a lawyer to handle the legal side of things. Of course, their situation was made much easier by the fact that they were in a very privileged position. The band was pretty much able to call the shots. Virgin Records were naturally very keen on making some money out of the band, and what a pleasant change it was for me to suddenly have an A&R department on my side of the fence, even if it was mostly just the press and publicity people at this stage.

Over the next few weeks I got to know John pretty well. His interests in music were similar to mine - certainly in the broadness of taste. We would spend a lot of time around at his place just listening to music. He had a fantastic collection of reggae; mostly early and mid '70's. He introduced me to the recordings of the Early Music Consort under David Munrow, their musical director before his suicide. Apart from Renaissance and Medieval music, folk music, especially Irish, was also a favourite with him. Current American black music was pretty much dominated by Disco at the time, and Donna Summer and Anita Ward, would also be present on the turntable. I would supplement the musical diet with tapes and discs from the more obscure reaches of my collection.

Apart from with John, I also felt particularly at ease with Dave Crowe who lived on the ground floor of the house, so most days I would make it over to Chelsea. I remember being a trifle bewildered at the relative lack of action, but assumed things would soon change. In fact after finishing the sessions in the Townhouse studios, we weren't to play music together until the recording of a Granada TV session in Manchester in mid June, almost two months later. Fortunately the organizer of the programme was Tony Wilson from Factory Records, who was very responsive to John's suggestion that maybe we could do a gig that night. Of course he had all the right connections and after a couple of phone calls a venue had been found - Russell's Club, later to become The Factory.

Pil at Russell's Club, Manchester 1979 (from left: Richard, Keith, Wobble & John)

I had a great time. The mood in the club was expectant to say the least, and amazingly the place was full, the Manchester grapevine having succeeded in spreading the word in just a few hours. In general up North, there was a distinct difference in attitude from that found down South, and I felt much more in sync with it. There was an underlying scepticism and people were less obsessed with the outward trappings: the length of your hair and the clothes you wore didn't seem have the same importance that they had in London.

As to the music, it was of course more like a rehearsal for us, the first we'd done in fact! But the informality of the event lent us the perfect opportunity to more or less relax and enjoy. We played mostly the new material that we had recorded on my joining, plus the "Public Image" song which I had never played before but which came off after a couple of false starts. I remember it being a real fun gig. Wobble, perched on the outsize barber's chair that we had brought up with us, had a broad grin on his face throughout, and John was in top skanking mode at the front of the stage. Keith's vacant expression was harder to decipher, but the audience reaction was clear.

We went down a storm, and I left Manchester with a very definite urge for more of the same. I knew that John and especially Wobble both felt as I did and were keen on doing more live work. The problem in this direction seemed to be Keith, and I think that quite simply, at this point in time anyway, he just didn't enjoy playing live. There were various attempts by Wobble to instigate a rehearsal, and once three of us even managed to appear at the same time in a rehearsal studio, but even that attempt came to nothing.

Despite the fact that it had been through Keith that I had joined the group, I soon found my relation with him deteriorating rapidly. It's a fact that within the Pil circle there was a heavy intake of speed and smoke, myself included, but Keith's predilection for stronger stimulants was another matter, and this probably affected the workings of the group as he was for me the main creative musical force behind the project. I was beginning to feel pretty frustrated by the whole affair. I have always loved playing just for the sake of playing, and doing live gigs is the logical extension of that, and here it was beginning to dawn on me that the huge potential of the band was being restricted by its inability to organize itself, as if the group's greatest asset was also its undoing. The spontaneous brilliance that could appear in a recording session was a very different quality from the more mundane attention to practical details that is also necessary for the day to day functioning of a band. My thrill at finding a successful group with no managerial interference would now be tempered by the realization that, with no one calling the shots, direction was erratic. In the whole of my time with Pil it is a fact that we had not one informal play or rehearsal session.

punter Richard, 1979

By mid summer, my involvement in the band would become little more than anecdotal. Apart from a night we spent in a studio down in Bermondsey when Wobble and I put down the rhythm track to "Graveyard" (also released on a single as "Another") the group's activity would be restricted to little more than promotion events.

There was one date when we were booked in to Virgin's Manor Studios in Oxfordshire, with the hope of recording more tracks for the album. Sad to say I remember the excursion more for the availability of the full sized snooker table, and the game I had trying to find a replacement for the exhaust pipe that had fallen off my car on our trip up the A 40. As for the recording, it was limited to just the laying down of some synth and guitar tracks from Keith, and a not very successful mixing session.

We did get to do some playing of sorts on a trip up to Newcastle. The Tyne & Tees channel programme "Check it Out" had a very strange notion of how to present Pop Culture current affairs. I assume it must have been a programme director with a thirst for notoriety who organized the debacle. From the moment we entered the studio it was pretty clear that something was not quite the way it should be. We played a song or two with no attention to our technical necessities from the studio hands, and when the interview started with the presenter and the four of us, it quickly became clear that we had been led in to a "Set Up".

Of course John was used to having to cope with the baggage from his past history in the Pistols, but this was a blatant attempt to create an "a la Grundy" live TV scandal. It was one thing for John to have to answer interminable questions about his past band, rather than the Pil project which he currently had going, but it was quite another to have to suffer the goading of an idiot who was trying to instigate an ugly on-screen scene. He nearly succeeded too! We left the set amongst a flurry of oaths, and lo and behold there was a posse of constables waiting backstage, no doubt pre-arranged by the channel to limit the damage we were supposed to wreak, and to add veracity to the headlines they were seeking!

This, in fact, was pretty much the typical response John would receive to his presence. People in the media generally would seize on the opportunity to create a scandal, or at least be more or less predisposed to the prospect of trouble. No wonder John's public image was abrasively protective, in contrast to the relatively placid private individual. I'll never forget the look of shock horror that spread over Joan Collins's face as she realized with whom she was sharing a backstage lift that was taking us up to the BBC studio for a Juke Box Jury programme!

If it were true that we didn't go overtly looking for trouble, I suppose at least, thank goodness, there was a strong element of unconventionality about the group. With the release of the single "Death Disco", The BBC was to provide the scenario for another promotional exercise in the shape of Top of The Pops. What a tacky programme that was, the norm, of course, being for acts to mime their respective song in "play-back" mode. To lend as much authenticity as possible to our intervention, John however had insisted on singing the vocal live. This meant that we had to record a backing track without voice in a BBC studio the night before.

Also on the show were The Psychedelic Furs and The Police. When on camera, they of course had their amps switched off, and the drummers used plastic cymbals and pads on the drums so that they could hear the backing track and mime to it with a certain degree of accuracy. This didn't appeal at all to us, and instead of turning our instruments off and letting John wail to the backing track, Wob and Keith decided to turn up their amps to full volume while I let rip on the drums. The result was, it must be admitted, pretty shambolic as we couldn't really keep in sync with what the viewers were hearing and seeing, and nor for that matter with John's voice. Still we had a great time, and I remember at least one of the studio technicians having a good laugh about the whole affair.

The summer trundled on still without any rehearsals or even time in the studio to try and finish the album, until finally a gig was arranged for the first edition of an independent Sci Fi Festival in a huge hanger up in Leeds. Despite the presence of a number of interesting groups including "Joy Division", the night for us was pretty awful with arguments within the band all day culminating in a row back stage and to cap it all an awful monitor sound when we finally came out on stage to play. John's reaction was to give his back to the audience for the duration of the set. I was fed up with the whole episode and when Keith started having a go at me when we came off stage as if it had all been my fault, that was it, I'd had enough. I was definitely not going to lie down and be the scapegoat for a crap gig. The following day I went over to Gunter Grove and put it to John: it was either Keith or me, but of course I knew the answer to that one, as there was no way John would give him the push. I had a final row with Keith, and that was the end of my stretch with Pil.

I was pretty sore at the way things had worked out, and in a fit of pique wrote a letter to the editor of the NME expressing "mutual satisfaction" blah blah at my exit, as well as having a dig at the band's lack of interest in playing live or even organizing a rehearsal. This was really setting myself up for a vitriolic response, and I was subsequently accused of being variously a "speed paranoiac", "a traitor to the cause" and of "being unable to keep time", apart from being subsequently ignored in the credits on release of the "Metal Box" album that appeared later that year.

In retrospect, I suppose I shouldn't have written the letter, but I'd seen and heard at first hand how the band had treated their previous ex-drummers and I just thought I'd be buggered if I'd let them do the same with me without getting my own oar in. Kid's stuff really, but it was interesting to read in a later interview with Keith that he thought I had never really believed that I was part of Pil, that somehow I was overawed by the experience. The opposite was nearer to the truth. I knew that the band was brimming with possibilities, for not only was there talent in abundance, but the time was absolutely right for them, they had a record company bending over backwards to accommodate them, and a late 70's public waiting for something original and authentic. But I also knew there were loads of other musicians out there with just as much talent and originality, but who would never have the breaks and the opportunity which Pil had. At the end of the day the Pop world is built on myths, and although most myths are built on some substance, once the myth is in place, Pop culture and its technocrats will see to the rest. Unless you really blow it of course.

Maybe I had a good excuse now for being well and truly despondent. On my first contact with them, I had seen Pil as embodying for me the perfect, independently-minded, alternative rock band; at the same time somehow representing the justification for my rejection of The Clash. So much for that theory.

Chapter 14 Back to School

During the previous months of relative inactivity I had renewed contact with Jim Whelton the bass player who I had seen playing with The Homosexuals earlier that Spring. He had been evicted from the Russell Square mansion, and had relocated to a squatted school house on the Shepherds Bush Road in Hammersmith. What a deliciously crazy ambience existed in that house. Its walls breathed an absolute irreverence to all standard mores combined with an almost feverish level of creative activity, and I found it the perfect antidote after the stultifying last few weeks I'd passed with Pil. There were seven or eight people living there, and each seemed obsessed with some crazy project or other. Uncluttered by doctrine and refreshingly un self-conscious, the place was a veritable factory of originality. Jim lived with Janey in a large, airy converted class room, where cans of paint, canvases, odd metal objects and strange wall hangings vied for space with Jim's double bass, trumpet, violin, and assorted percussive objects.

It was a wild and quirky world, where you would never know what to expect next, but as an overall impression what comes to my mind is COLOUR. You might be wondering what on earth I mean by that, but memory sometimes functions in strange ways, and the most vivid memory that I retain of those days is of an overriding presence of bright blues, pinks, yellows, greens. It was as if the monochrome that had been the recent underlying scheme of all things punk had been blown away in a swirl of colour. Apart from improvised musical sessions, on calling in to the place it would be no surprise if you were to find yourself part of one of Otto's spontaneous theatre sketches or an unwitting participator in someone's super-8 short, and the banquets were an event not to be missed.

Straight out of the set for Buñuel's "Viridiana" supper-scene, held in the school canteen complete with full length trestle-tables, up to 30 odd bods would descend out of the night. Candelabras would light a phantasmagorical spread of food and drink as mutts would compete for scraps from the floor between your feet. Light entertainment would be provided from a variety of sources, the floor being available to anyone who wanted to perform. Inevitably as the night progressed the party would develop along its own unscripted, alcohol imbibed path, and more than once we would haul out instruments, even if my percussion would have to be provided by a selection of pots, pans and various items of ironmongery.

I was to participate in various projects with Jim, who I always found the most creative and open of musical cohorts. His taste in music was wide and of a varied complexion. As with me, Jazz was up there high amongst his loves, but in an unstudied, un-academic way. He was a great fan of Ornette Coleman and Charlie Parker and I still play cassette tapes that he made up for me with their music and other latin tracks that he would unearth and then proceed to mix in a his own inimitable way. What you could be sure of with Jim, was that he would not be tied down to any pre-conceived concept, and he would never allow things to remain in a comfortable "familiar" groove.

I'm loathe to use the word eccentric with its connotations of wild madness, because Jim's was such a sharp wit, but to describe him as unconventional neither does him justice! When I arrived at the School House, his band The Homosexuals were in their last throes. I met the other members Anton and Bruno a couple of times, but Jim made it clear that the band was finished and he wanted to start something new.

The first project we got together was with John Glyn, the sax player I had played with off and on in The Bank of Dresden. Jim also knew him, and we decided to use the rehearsal space that John had in his house in Shepherd's Bush. With Jim on bass and John on tenor, we supplemented the band with Tim, a friend of John and wizard on the accordion.

Jim The Bass

We started producing some great tunes with heavy-funky rhythms, searing sax from John, and an interesting and unusual sound with Tim's contribution, and then found just the soulful voice we were looking for from the throat of Michelle. Within a couple of weeks we were recording songs in a place that was to become a regular haunt – Surrey Sounds, a studio owned by the brother of Chris, one of the occupants of the school house. It was to become a second home to Jim who thrived behind the controls of the mixing desk, and was to use the studio for enumerable projects over the next few years. Unfortunately though, the band was short lived. Michelle was taken ill, other projects surfaced and all that remained of the "Nameless Band" was a small collection of songs we had recorded.

John and Tim went on to form a successful salsa/African based group The Republic, with who I played a couple of times when their regular drummer was out of action. Jim and I carried on with sporadic collaborations. One highlight for me was the recording of "C'est Fab" with Nancy Sesay and the Melodairs. A typical Jim production mixing out-of-tune falsetto vocals with a driving rhythm and thick horn section. Gigs were not a common occurrence, but when they did materialize they were inevitably of the strangest sort. I remember one up in Luton, held at a squatted complex in the centre of the town. True to form, it was more of a "happening" than an ordinary gig: there was theatre and spontaneous painting, and I do remember that we attracted a lot of un-appreciative attention from neighbours and police.

I was happy to play around with a number of groups over the next few months, although in this mode there was no way I could make a living. After a bit of economic stability with Pil, I was back to having to scrape a living from somewhere, and luckily was offered a part time job by my old friend Avo. A few hours a week looking after the paper work for his growing stage lighting company allowed us to live in the pretty basic way to which Esperanza and I were accustomed, while giving me plenty of time to play. I've already mentioned the band "The Vincent Units" that our neighbour Neal Brown had formed. This had now evolved into a similarly styled ensemble - "The Tesco Bombers". Derek, Nick and I would variously take our turn on the drum stool, and at one gig with them I even played an old double bass that I had recently acquired.

Another little project that I had going at the time was with a jazz Big Band organized by the Morley School of music, down in Lambeth. A friend had told me they were short of a drummer, so not without a certain amount of apprehension I presented myself and kit at the college one evening. I'd never played in a "proper" jazz band before, so I took it as a challenge to learn the new rhythms that were expected of me. I thoroughly enjoyed it, they had a hot ten piece horn section with good soloists, and after a few rehearsals we did a couple of gigs – one in the Maudsley Hospital, South London. Unfortunately my stint with them came to a sudden and almost violent end. The rehearsal studio we were allocated was on the third floor of the college, to which I would have to single-handed haul my drums. The presence of a lift was obviously a great help, so imagine my horror when the director of the college ran over to me as I was loading in my gear, forbidding me to use a facility supposedly reserved only for invalids and emergencies. The tutor of the big band wasn't up to confronting his boss, so in an angry scene I said adios to my short-lived jazz experience.

*

It was around this time that I was to hitch up with Joe for the first time since the end of "The 101'ers". It was Mole, our original bass player with whom I had re-made regular contact including the occasional stand-in drumming session for his band "Pitiful", who was the main instigator of the event. We called ourselves the "Soul Vendors" so you can imagine the musical fare that we offered. Derek also played some drums, Inigo and someone else on saxes, Tim on accordion, and Rowena the lead singer with the "Modettes" on vocals. "Ain't Too Proud to Beg" was one of the covers that we did, along with other Tamla faves. The gig, which was probably a benefit of some kind, was held in a packed Tabernacle, a community centre in Powis Square just off the Portobello Rd, and it was a great feeling to be playing again with my two old mates. Joe was now living back in the neighbourhood in Lancaster Rd, and we would see each other from time to time. It was as if he had come back to earth again after a couple of years in I'm not sure what place. As far as I was concerned the hatchet had finally been buried.

Soul Vendors, Tabernacle 1980. (Joe, Mole, & Richard with Derek & Nick behind)

My renewed contact with Joe gave impetus to a venture that I'd had in the back of my mind for some time. "The 101'ers" had released just one single, with "Keys to Your Heart" on the A side, back in 1976, but there were more studio tracks and live tapes hanging around, and I knew there was sufficient material for a "posthumous" album.

It would have been at an earlier date than the period of which I'm currently writing that word had got around that I was toying with the idea of a 101'ers album. Can you imagine Bernie Rhodes, the manager of "The Clash", actually having the cheek to come down to my basement flat, accompanied by Mickey Foote who'd no doubt been cajoled in to showing Bernie where I lived? I politely invited them in, and was then left flabbergasted as Bernie let forth in the way that only he could, giving me not one good reason why there should be no 101'ers album release. As ever with Bernie, it was a one way conversation, and I ended up literally grabbing him by his lapels and throwing him out of the front door, with him screaming blue murder at me, and that I'd live to regret it etc ...

Why was it that Bernie was so keen on preventing the disc? His main argument, with me at least, was that the band and what it had done had been irrelevant. But if that were so, why should he even bother to take the trouble of coming down to my flat to argue the point? From the start of "The Clash" it was clear that Bernie would have preferred it if "The101'ers" had never existed, and that the only Clash precursor, despite the fact that that they had only ever actually performed a couple of gigs, had been the "London S.S.", Mick Jones's previous group, with which of course Bernie had been involved as manager.

I think his main problem was simply his paranoia at having "his" Joe associated with a group that didn't fit in to the image/ideology that he had constructed so carefully for "The Clash". In the first years of The Punk Phenomenon his mind was so obsessed with ideas of "Punks" and "Hippies", "those with us" and "those against us", that I don't think he could stomach the idea of a photo of Joe in the press with long side burns playing a Chuck Berry tune......after all, at the start of the "Uprising" it was precisely against these things that the new movement had been built.

This episode, as you might imagine, did nothing more than increase my resolve to complete the project. By early 1980 after the renewed contact between us, Joe was behind the idea, and working with Mole we set out a plan of action. The first step was to locate the recordings and make sure we had sufficient material for an album. This was relatively easy. I contacted Jackson's studios in Rickmansworth where we had recorded our first session with Vic Maile. There would be no problem there and they sent us a copy of the tracks. The BBC sessions that we had recorded in Maida Vale were also easily available. Through Clive we spoke to Mike Robinson who had engineered the sessions, and we obtained not only masters but also the multitracks. What happened with the songs Roger Armstrong had produced for Chiswick in Pathway studios remains a mystery to me. They would have been simple to include in the album, but for some reason we used only "Sweet Revenge" from those sessions. I can maybe understand why we preferred to use our unreleased BBC recorded version of "Keys to Your Heart", but I have no idea why we should have decided to leave out "Rabies (from the dogs of love)". One possible explanation is that Chiswick let us have the use of "Sweet Revenge" as a straight swop for us having let them use "5* Rock'n'Roll" on the B side of the first single four years previously. Another is that maybe they preferred to keep "Rabies" as an exclusive track for a single on their label. In fact, they did later release a seven inch single on Ace Records, coinciding with the release of our album.

The other source for material was a box of cassettes that Mickey Foote dug out from the bottom of his wardrobe. These were quite a revelation, and I remember the first time Joe and I listened to them we realized that, despite their deficient sound quality, the power of the band cut through, and some would definitely be usable. Mickey, as sound man with the band, had adopted the sensible practise of recording all the gigs, although on occasions he had had to record over a previous gig if he hadn't ben able to buy a new cassette! They were only really meant as a reference, and we would usually listen to them in the van after the show, during the long haul back home. They had been recorded on cassette, usually with one channel through the mixing desk and the other live through a mike so their quality left much to be desired. However, there were a couple of tapes that stood out, and we decided to use just one source to keep the sound quality, at least on the live material, as even as possible. The recording that we plumped for was a Roundhouse gig when we had supported VanderGraaf Generator in April '76. The high domed ceiling of the old engine shed gave a natural reverb to the sound that we preferred to the drier sound on some other tapes, and you could at least hear the four instruments and voices. Actually I'm still rather fond of the sound to this day, and interestingly Joe was later to refer to our version of Bo Didley's "Don't Let Go" taken from the Roundhouse gig, as the best thing on the album.

Having located the material the rest of the project was relatively simple. The first thing we decided was that we should split any resulting income six ways, equally shared between Mole, Dan, Clive, Mickey, Joe and myself, thus avoiding any possible arguments as to who should get what percentage.

Mole in the studio…1981

Incredibly, this arrangement we also extended to the publishing income, so all original songs that hadn't been previously registered were to be credited to the six of us. This was cooperativism taken to an extreme! Secondly, we decided to create our own record label. We hadn't even started to tout it around, so it seemed a sensible decision, as most of the material was ours anyway. For a name Joe and I came up with "Andalucia Records". It seemed an apt eulogy to the two Andalucian sisters, Esperanza and Paloma, we had both loved during the duration of the group's existence, and in a strange way symbolized the romantic memories we both shared of the best times of the group.

The next stage in the process was to find a record company interested in distributing the album, and again I didn't have much problem. In my recent stint with Pil I'd got to know a few people in the Virgin set up, and it was easy to arrange a meeting with Simon Draper, then director of A&R. He was very enthusiastic, and allowed us to organize it the way we wanted. We kept control of all aspects of the production, leaving Virgin to manufacture, distribute, and help out on the promotion. So that was it, everything was more or less in place. Joe, Mole Mickey and I went down to Surrey Sounds studio with Chris and decided on the final selection of tracks, their order and as much improvement as we could conjure up for the live stuff, while transferring it from cassette to the ¼ inch master.

While all this was going on I'd had a call from someone at Island Records on behalf of a group looking for a drummer, and from the resulting meeting I became temporarily too busy to carry on with the album, and I left Mole to sort out the artwork side of things in my absence.

*

"Basement Five" was the group I went to see, and with a recently recorded album due out on Island, they had been offered an extensive tour supporting Ian Dury and the Blockheads, but were without a drummer. Their music was interesting enough, but I made it clear from the start that I'd do the tour with them up until Xmas and then review the situation.

Dennis Morris, the leader and singer was an accomplished photographer, and had been involved in that role with Lydon at various times. Not surprisingly, given his professional background, he was very much aware of the "publicity" side of things, and the first thing he did after I'd accepted the drum stool was to run off a publicity photo shoot in the Basing Street studios, and then send out press releases with "Dudanski – Ex Pil" all over them. In fact Dennis was pretty much obsessed with the whole Pil phenomenon to the extent that even the music could be described as being "Pilesque". Despite their Jamaican backgrounds, the music being played veered away from reggae, much nearer to "wall of sound/heavy metal/doom rock". The whole project for me was saved by the cavernous bass of Leo and inventive guitar of J. R. That, and the fact that I thoroughly enjoyed their company.

Once again I was with a band that seemed to command an inordinate amount of respect from "The Biz". Knowing the right people of course meant so much in getting your foot in the door, like in every other walk of life I suppose, but it did rile me that there were so many talented musicians out there who just didn't get the same look-in as others with much less to offer. We spent a lot of time hanging around the Island offices in Chiswick, but maybe that's not surprizing, as it was here that we had our rehearsal room. We must have done some playing together before the tour, although in fact the music's structure was very simple. I would only really have to link with Leo's bass, as J. R. used his guitar more to weave a sheet of sound through an amazing array of effects pedals, while Dennis would wail over the top.

One advantage of being associated with the Island set up was its proximity to fine reggae. I got hold of as many catalogue albums as I could and had no problem in finding concert tickets when there was something interesting. One night there was a memorable Toots and the Maytals gig at Hammersmith Palais. What a surprise next day as we were asked to accompany as many girls from the offices as could be mustered to the basement studio in St Peter's Square. There we found Toots with a huge bag of ganja and as much whisky and champagne as we could handle. The previous night's concert had been recorded for a prospective live album, and someone had decided that a bit more crowd response noise was needed. A party mood was assured, and I'm sure the producer got as much cheering and screaming as he asked for. I wasn't aware that the album had ever been released until one day, nearly twenty five years later, I walked in to the office of a label manager at Universal in L.A., and there it was sitting on his desk: a re-edition of Toots Live at Hammersmith Palais – 1980! I must confess: I asked him to put it on, intrigued as I was to know if any of our screaming had been used!

The serious business started when we set off on the autumn tour. We needed a sound man on the desk out front so I contacted Mickey Foote, who agreed to do the tour but then, just before we left, I had a run in with Dennis. It was to be just one more of those little ironies that seem to run throughout this tale. With Pil I had played on an album and then been left off the credits; with Basement Five the exact opposite occurred - I was put on the credits when I shouldn't have been! Charlie Charles had in fact done the session with them just before I had joined, as of course Dennis knew very well. Chatting to Charlie later on during the tour I felt it necessary to explain that I'd known nothing about the credits business. He was a really gentle geezer, and of course didn't give a monkey's, but the detail had left a bad taste in my mouth. Thank goodness it was the Blockheads with who we were on tour, because I must admit I got pretty bored with the music we were playing. Night after night sitting on my drum stool, listening to the platitudes of Dennis started to get to me, but "Ian Dury and the Blockheads" was such a great band. The first time I'd seen Dury was with "Kilburn and The Highroads" in 1973, appropriately up on Kilburn High Road at "The Cock", and "The 101'ers" had done a couple of support gigs with him in 1975. His style was very much in place in those early pre-punk days, with his barrow-boy banter and no-bullshit theatricality. There were many "older generation" acts that had tweaked their image (and their music) to fall in line with the new world created by punk post-1976, but that's an observation that cannot be made of Dury who had always had his own distinctive identity.

Basement 5. Dennis, Leo, Richard & J.R. (1980)

In fact his music and style at the time of the Kilburns was most definitely ahead of its time. Typically, when recording the "New Boats and Panties" album in '76/'77, he would create a much more elastic feel, more akin to funk than to the punk thrashing that was the order of the day.

In 1980 the band as a live act was just about at its peak. The rhythm section of Norman Watt Roy and Charlie Charles was colossal. Davey Payne had always been one of my favourite horn blowers on the circuit, and to top it all Ian had guesting with him Don Cherry on trumpet and Wilko Johnson on guitar. A luxury band indeed! The dates, at what appeared to be all the two to four thousand capacity halls in England and Scotland, were pretty much back to back over a couple of months, and we got in to the drudge of a typical tour routine: bus – sound check – hotel – gig – booze – hotel – bus ... ad infinitum. It was just as well that in the band there were a couple of pool freaks apart from me, and "three-coin spoof" became the method for deciding who was to pay the next round of drink. The presence of Wilko was much appreciated by me. What a pleasure it was to have a chat with him on our own at a quiet corner table of the hotel restaurant. Always with an interesting and original angle on things, and once on the subject of the English Romantic poets.... no stopping him!

The tour ended but I had decided way before that I'd had enough. Not to say that the project couldn't have become successful: it was just that it didn't convince me. There was one concert booked over the New Year at the I.C.A on the Mall. I didn't want them to have to pull it, so that was the last gig I did with them. Leo I bumped in to later when he was working in Mick Jones's post Clash B.A.D. outfit. Dennis and J.R. I haven't seen since.

Chapter 15   Breakdown and Away

I was now once again able to devote myself full time to "The 101'ers" album. I finished negotiating the deal with Virgin and we set a release date for the end of March, 1981. Mole had organized all the design work. We had decided on a down beat, black and white presentation, with typewriter lettering. We used photos of the band taken by Jules on the back cover, and on the front a simple black and white pic of a local hobo character that frequented the pavements and alleys around All Saints Road and Portobello. He was known to us as "The Metal Eater" as invariably he would be chewing on one of the many metal objects that he had hanging from his bedraggled clothing. He had problems with his legs and you would find him sprawled on the sidewalk. Conversation would be limited, but we all knew his favourite food – chicken legs from the local take away. Not on the same plane as most of us he was, like Vivian the bag lady from Westbourne Grove, another representative of the nameless uncounted that inhabited the no man's land of our bustling city. These were the real outcasts, usually without family, no decent place to sleep, scarce means, and with mental problems that in some cases were perhaps all that protected them from the big city madness that surrounded them. We thought the Metal Eater an ideal character to represent the album and it was left to Joe, who else, to come up with the title. "ELGIN AVENUE BREAKDOWN" was an inspired invention, made more attractive by its working on various levels. Elgin Avenue was of course the main thoroughfare through the Maida Hill neighbourhood where the band had started. "Breakdown" had the double meaning of "stoppage" and "summary", while it also related to the Metal Eater image beneath it.

Mole had the idea of giving away a free poster with the first 500 copies, and proceeded to design, again in black and white, a rather disturbing collage where the images related obliquely to the titles of the album songs.

Portobello Opera Busker (Inspiration for Bramley's poster)

There were more band photos and info on the reverse side. Another large size poster was also organized for pasting in the street. This was designed and screen printed by our friend Simon Bramley, and again we returned to the theme used on the album cover. This time we used the image of a little old lady who for years could be seen on the Portobello market with her pram stacked with a dansette gramophone and a stash of scratchy opera records. This very original DJ / Busker would find a spot on the road where the booming bass of dub, which was of course the predominant music to be heard down Portobello, wouldn't interfere with the plaintive screeching of her favourite arias, and hope a few pennies would be dropped in the hat.

The logo for the record label was adapted from an original poster that Joe had designed for the band's stint at "The Elgin" pub, and with the album liner notes wittily written by Neal Brown of The Vincent Units, the album was ready to go. It had all been an unbelievably smooth operation and our album reached the shops with neither a bang nor a whimper in March. Through Virgin we organized some basic promo and in the music press of the day the album received prominent reviews, all, from what I can remember, extremely positive.

Melody Maker was interested in doing an in depth interview and Joe, Mole and I made the appointment at Mole's flat in All Saint's Road. It was a very relaxed affair as we reminisced and joked about the old days. With this I felt at last "The 101'ers" could be laid to rest. For better or worse the album fairly reflected the bands output, and its position as one of the more interesting groups in the immediate pre-punk panorama. But perhaps more important than that, it had brought together old friends without any rancour or squabbling, and enabled us to savour again the special times we had shared. The record, with just a few thousand copies sold, was certainly no great money spinner, but that hadn't been the point. In fact, the disc was deleted after four years and was never re-released, although in time it has become a bit of a collector's piece.

Having worked on the record with Mole, we continued to collaborate on a number of projects. One was a busking excursion to Paris that we organized with a group of friends. It was a pretty crazy set up with Mole on guitar, Sanja on bass, myself on drums, Little Richard guitar and trumpet, and Chris an American girl singer. Our selection of tunes was extremely varied, with a sprinkling of Mole originals and obscure covers, including a version of the Antonio C. Jobim samba "Uma Nota So" when I had the chance to practise my Portuguese in singing mode. After a few days rehearsal, we set off on the train with the minimum amount of equipment - myself with just a high-hat and snare, and the guitars with "Mighty Atom" battery guitar amps. Richard had previously been living in Paris, and knew the best street pitches for playing, although there was a ferocious competition for them amongst what appeared to be very professional looking groups in comparison to our bedraggled unit. It seemed as if most of the day would be spent wandering the streets looking for a reasonable spot to set up the gear. In some places we would hardly make enough for a cup of coffee, and at others we would attract a semi-enthusiastic crowd, and enough cash to pay for a meal. In one narrow street on the left bank I received a drenching. An upper floor window suddenly opened, and sitting on my drum stool, I was unable to avoid a bucket of water thrown by the irate neighbour. We got in to all kinds of scrapes, including a run in with police in the metro for jumping the barriers, and problems with the Algerian owners of the dormitory room that we all piled into for the night. It was just as well that we found the large soup kitchens, frequented mostly by Senegalese immigrants, where a solid meal could be obtained for just a few francs. After four or five days we were broke, and our very enjoyable little Parisian adventure came to a premature end.

Bramley's street poster

During the time spent working on "Elgin Avenue Breakdown", I had also been working at Pil over the matter of royalties. When I had joined the band two years previously, the agreement had been that apart from a nominal weekly wage I would also be entitled to a share of the publishing. This was generous but also reflected the way we had actually recorded the songs. The fact that my name hadn't appeared on the album credits made the process more difficult, but finally John signed a letter confirming my co-authorship of the songs I had recorded in the studio with them. With this letter and the go ahead from Pil's lawyer I was able to sign a collection deal with Virgin Publishing. This was all very good news to me, and suddenly I was presented with a cheque the likes of which I'd never had before. Esperanza and I knew exactly what we wanted to do with the cash.

Over the years I had developed a bit of a romantic obsession with Brazil. It had started as a ten year old on reading the biography of an early 20th century explorer, Colonel Fawcett, who was eventually engulfed without trace by the Amazonian jungle after various years of confrontations with anacondas, piranhas, fevers, undiscovered Indian tribes and the like.

My interest had been re-kindled through its music, and in particular after I had stumbled across a couple of great "Lyrichord" albums with recordings of Candomblé religious songs from Salvador in Bahia, and cult music from Belem, the port-city at the mouth of the Amazon. Many of the folk music recordings that I bought around that time would, not surprisingly, have leanings towards the percussive side of things, and this lead to an interest in recordings of cult "spirit possession" music, whether Asian, African, or in particular from Cuba, Haiti and Brazil. This being, of course, during the pre-internet era, I did a bit of investigating in the library of the School of Oriental and African Studies in London, and from there realized that Bahia was the place I wanted to visit.

Salvador, state capital of the province of Bahia, had been the original Portuguese imperial capital of Brazil, before Brasilia, before Rio de Janeiro, and it was to this area in the North East of the country that huge numbers of slaves had been taken to work the sugar plantations. Their descendants had maintained the religious traditions of the Yoruba and Fon people from modern day Nigeria, and the ritual music and dance that is practiced today in the many cult houses of the area, forms the basis of ceremonies in which it is believed the initiates become possessed by deities of the Yoruba pantheon.   As well as this interest in Brazilian popular religion, I was also attracted by its popular music, so rich in rhythm and melody, yet for me at this time still relatively unknown when compared to the music from its giant neighbour to the North. From the start I was quite clear in that given the choice between a prolonged visit to either Brazil or the States, it was the former that interested me more. I suppose such a decision had a lot to do with a certain rejection of the all-encompassing, world dominating North American culture. Despite the love that I had for particularly black American music, culturally speaking Brazil was just so much more fascinating to me at the time. American hegemony in just about everything was enough for me to reject it in favour of something of which I knew relatively little; this and the reality of its Latin roots, as opposed to the Anglo basis of U.S. American culture.

I decided to start learning Portuguese, and through Brazilian friends in London made contact with their family in Rio de Janeiro. Our original idea was to move up to the North East as soon as possible, but we made such good friends in Rio that we delayed our plans. For over a month Esperanza and I were the guests of Estela at her flat in Ipanema, having arrived to the city in the Autumn of '81. What a fantastic place and it didn't take us long to fall absolutely in love with the country and its people. Music was everywhere. It permeated every part of the place: on the buses, in a ticket office, on the beach, in a supermarket, someone next to you would be singing a tune or tapping out a bossa beat. It sounds awfully hackneyed, but it's a fact. Brazil had (and I imagine still has) an absolute obsession with music, and it seemed in such a natural, unforced way, crossing over class and age. The hard lines between what back home would be defined as different pop music genres such as folk music, or rock or soul, did not seem to have the same relevance, and even the pop stars appeared to retain a connection with their public that you would just not see in the UK. Why and how this unity within plurality of Brazil's musical culture had come about I can't explain. It's easier to understand why it should be so in a smaller country, like say Cuba, but its interesting that it could be possible in a modern country of nearly 200 million people.

Sergio was our indefatigable host. With him we immersed ourselves in the magical Rio night life of dance-halls and clubs followed by lazy days sipping chá on the sands of Copacabana beach. He introduced me to some musicians and having sat in on a couple of rehearsals we accompanied the group for a gig to Juiz de Fora in the nearby province of Minas Gerais. "Rogerio's Skylab" was the name of the band, which played a kind of Bowie influenced

Bossa - Rock. However, our sights were set on Bahia and we finally booked our seats on the long coach journey up to Salvador.

We had no contacts in the city, and as was to be our way for the next eight months, we moved around the cheapest hotels until we found one that we liked. Salvador was very different from Rio. Gone was the sophisticated Copacabana chic, replaced by a much more down to earth reality. Of the 80% black population, over 50% were unemployed, and you noticed a hardship on the streets as much as the easy going friendliness of the people. Apart from a more modern commercial area by the port, the city was a sprawling mass of mostly ramshackle housing occupying the slopes of the various hills it straddled. Even the more affluent neighbourhoods would be overshadowed by the inevitable favela on an adjacent hillside. In the early 80's the city's potential as an exotic destination on western tour operators' lists was still to be realized.

Batucada Bahia

The picturesque though crumbling central Pelourinho district, named after the whipping post once situated on its square, had yet to receive the attentions of the restorers and speculators, and here and elsewhere in the city the decrepit remains of its colonial past merely hinted at its former affluence, when it had been the capital of the world's largest sugar producing area.

Our real introduction to Bahia was made after a few days when we went along with the suggestion of an acquaintance to attend a street party in a neighbourhood nearby. Street party was a partly correct description, as it turned out in fact to be a rehearsal session of one of Salvador's principle samba bands – "Ile-Aiye" from the barrio of Liberdade. As we approached the rehearsal area among the crowds of revellers on their way to the party, passing the old ladies by the side of the road selling home-prepared bottles of batida (cachaça and fruit juice) from makeshift stalls, the throb of the bass drums gained in volume sending my heart to my mouth, transporting me back to the same feeling I had once had as a child. The same thrilling sensation but in very different circumstances.

In 1950's England, the remnants of Britain's empire days were still just about hanging by a thread. Because of its position in the Thames estuary, the Isle of Sheppey, my birthplace, had always been of strategic importance for the protection of London upstream, and the nearby naval docks on the Medway. It had developed through the centuries as a controlling point for the upper English Channel. Its history as a naval and military garrison went back to the 14th century and beyond, but especially after the Dutch had actually attacked and occupied the place in 1695. Relics from this maritime past lie scattered through my childhood memories like the flotsam and jetsam we would sift through on the pebbly beaches. The sunken, ammunition–carrying wreck, lying with its masts still visible on a sand bank just off the Sheerness coast, with its huge cargo of dynamite still a potential threat to us, its nearby neighbours. The still surviving row of Georgian houses close by the quay at Queenborough, from where Nelson's Lady Hamilton would have waited for her admiral's return, gazing out over the muddy river Swale and its creeks to the misty marshes of tree-less

Deadman's Isle. What an aptly named place that is, as it was the never-to-leave drop off point for disease-ridden sailors bound for London who had been diagnosed with the plague, cholera or some other such horror. Later in the 60's, Radio Caroline and other "Pirate" radio stations would use the abandoned, 2nd World War observation towers that remained standing close to the coast, and here again "pirate" was a very appropriate naming as this had been prime smuggling territory with its proximity to Europe and its maze of fog-bound creeks indenting its shoreline.

The memory that the Ile-Aiye bass drums had awakened in me was that of a small child standing on the pavement of Marine Parade, Sheerness, on what would have almost certainly been a blustery summer's carnival day. Attention to my candy floss was entirely superseded not so much by the spectacle of the massed marching Royal Marine band with its twirling standard bearer up front, but by the pounding beat of a monster drum, still invisible around the corner. What set my heart racing to the point of bursting was a short fat man bedecked with a huge leopard skin, upon which was strapped an enormous bass drum bigger than its owner. The excitement increased with its gradual approach till it was almost unbearable, and on passing I was left with a tingling sensation and a sense of almost disbelief in what I had just heard!

Little did we know, but our arrival in Bahia had been well timed. With carnival usually at the end of Feb or beginning of March, the summer holiday period would start at Christmas. Each neighbourhood of the city would have its own samba band, or Bloco, and in preparation for carnival there would be a ten week period of weekend rehearsals. What this translates to is two month's partying, with numerous bands playing all over the city. Some would play in the afternoon, such as the "Kalifas do Baghdad"; "Ile-Aiye" would start at eleven at night and go on till after sunrise. Entry was free, and money would be made on the nearby bar. The frenetic party pace would heat up the nearer it came to carnival as, apart from the weekend rehearsals, each neighbourhood would also celebrate its own particular fiesta which would usually last for three or four days. What I am describing here is two months partying on a gigantic scale!

"Afoshe" or "Batucada", terms used to describe the music made by samba bands, is a most direct descendent from Brazil's African past. The groups consist of typically twenty, thirty or more drummers. At the rear, often with older more experienced players, were the massed ranks of bass drums or "surdos". Beaten with a single large padded stick, the other hand being is used to dampen the skin and "bend" the note. Next came medium sized drums "repenique" and then the snare drummers towards the front. There would also be the higher pitched "tamborims" and various sized cuicas which would both be used in a more soloist role. The cuica is a fantastic instrument producing a rhythmic screech or song by pulling on a wooden stick attached to the inner surface of the drum skin. The bass cuicas could have a twisting horn system resting on the player's shoulder to help project the sound. Again, the pitch of the note produced is controlled by pressure from the other hand on the outer surface of the skin.

The ensemble director would face the band out front and conduct proceedings with the help of a simple whistle. An almost non stop rhythmic blowing which blended with the overall sound of the group, yet kept a tight control over every nuance of the music. The rhythmic power created by such a band just defies description. And imagine that this would continue all night, with each theme lasting up to forty minutes or more. To this totally acoustic music there would also be added a vocal element on microphone. There is a long tradition of song writing specifically for the carnival leading to a competition with a "best lyrics" category, where the lyricists would often reflect on contemporary problems or comment on local anecdotes, often in a light-hearted manner. A relatively recent development when we were there in '82, was the influence of reggae-style toasting, with maybe a heavy dub echo on the vocal.To this incredible musical event, we mustn't forget the audience, although audience isn't really the most apt description. Here was punter-participation to a high degree, not really surprising as the Blocos were community based neighbourhood bands. There would be certain fluidity in the composition of the group throughout the night, and a coming and going of percussionists playing a variety of cow-bells, gourds, gongs, shakers and almost anything that would make a noise. The adeptness of Brazilians in producing percussive instruments from any old object, and to play them at the most unexpected moment, was one of the first things that had struck me on arrival. And then we have the spectacle of the typical samba dance with its graceful, rapid foot shuffle .... and above all the absolute disposition of the people to have a good time. The original samba called "Chula" or "Samba de Roda" was named after the simple idea of a circle of people who each in turn would enter the circle and do their turn... This was still very much the way people enjoyed their night out with the Blocos.

What can I say about the people of Liberdade that we met that first night? Within no time we were being treated as two more of the family, and my enduring impression was related to the fact that here we were the only two white faces in a sea of black. Liberdade was not a favela but it was most definitely a poor working class area with a huge population nearing half a million. The contrast with London was marked. I had been in many similar situations, black clubs and shebeens of which there were many in our Notting Hill area, where you would be accepted so long as you were buying your can of Red Stripe, but usually with more than a hint of wariness. In these circumstances Whitey on Blackman's territory was the basic vibe in London or elsewhere in Britain, and not surprisingly, given the underlying colour prejudice that exists in British society. Here that attitude did not exist, and interestingly we should find it to be so in Liberdade, which we would later discover had the reputation for being the most politically "radical" of the Salvador Blocos, where "black pride" awareness had its greatest following. The whole question of racism in Brazil is a difficult subject. As I've said, coming from Britain there did not seem to be anything like the same tension, and besides, intermarriage between whites, blacks and Indians down the centuries had produced a mestizo population where the issue of colour seemed an irrelevance. However, with time we realized the picture was not quite so simple. Statistics show a most definite cultural divide into white middle class and black poor with, not surprisingly, an even greater distinction between races when it came to the power brokers in politics and the upper echelons of business.

We were taken "under the wing" of a group of friends who could not do enough for us. We were invited to numerous households and parties, and they helped us find a house with a spare room we could rent. It was situated in the Santo Antonio neighbourhood not far from Pelourinho, and it worked out fine for us. Liberdade remained, however, our "home" barrio, and as the carnival season grew in impetus we would inevitably make our way around the different barrios and Blocos with Naomi, Cabral and co. The fiesta in the Vermelho district was one of the most colourful when people pile into flower-decked boats and pay homage to the goddess of the sea: Yemenja. The fiesta of Lavagem do Bonfim, was another special event with the white clad Bahiana ladies leading the procession in honour of el Senhor do Bonfim - Lord of the Good Ending! All of these events were naturally accompanied by the ever presence of infinite number of Batucada drum music groups, which would then coalesce at the end of the day into a night long party.

The evident symbiosis between the ancestral African religions and the adopted Catholic faith results in a fascinating combination. It is difficult sometimes to work out whether the object of veneration is, as for example in the Bonfim festa, Oxalá from the Yoruba pantheon or Christ from the Catholic, because Brazilians demonstrate such a great facility for transferring the characteristics of God to Saint and vice versa. The hierarchy of the Brazilian catholic church, maybe simply because of the fervour demonstrated by the "converted", seems to have taken a pragmatic stance on the phenomenon, which in Europe would I think have been unequivocally condemned as heresy! All you had to do was enter a church during a service to witness the incredible intensity of religious feeling of the people. It seems pretty obvious that behind this process, for the enslaved blacks it had been a mechanism available for them to retain a connection with their ancestral Gods and culture.

A similar process is at work in the development of the Bahiano dance form – Capoeira. It does not need much imagination to see in its origins a form of violent combat, similar to the marshal arts of China and Japan. A prohibition on all forms of fighting was strictly enforced by the Portuguese slave-owners, and the evolution into

Capoeira was the result, dancing being considered a lesser threat to the white man's power.

The music accompanying Capoeira dance, with its variety of drums and the one-stringed berimbau with its "wow-wow" sound created by an open gourd played against the stomach of the player, though obviously derived from Africa is particular to Bahia. In fact the number of popular musical forms in Brazil is incredibly varied, each region having its own identity. One style of music popular at carnival, with its origins in the southern cities of Rio and Sao Paolo, was the Trio Electrico. They had developed in the 1960's and relied on a manic march-time rhythm overlaid with soaring electric guitars. The speed at which the music was played produced a jumping mass in the following crowds, not dissimilar to the pogoing fans at the early punk concerts, as the Trios would play from the back of a lorry winding its way through the streets. It was a very different music compared to the funkier beat of the Bloco and Afoxé massed bands. We heard and saw yet another variation of Brazilian folk carnival music on a journey we made to the interior of the Bahia State to a sleepy ex-mining town called Lençois. Sleepy that is, until a local marching band took to the streets to celebrate the local patron saint. The sound of this group was based on simple straight flutes (many played by kids) and of course drums, and what a fantastic music they produced! The town was also interesting for its colonial style architecture. In the mid 19th century diamonds had been discovered in the local river bed, and the subsequent "rush" of prospectors had created sudden wealth for some, but I am pretty sure that it was in this town that I picked up something that was to drastically alter my stay in Bahia.

*

Back in Salvador, we had been invited to a party, but I was not feeling too good and had no appetite whatsoever. An observant elderly gent sidled up to me, commented that I did not seem to be very hungry, asked me to look him in the eyes and proceeded to diagnose, with total certainty, that I had hepatitis. The next day I had a blood test that turned out positive, and was subsequently informed by a doctor friend that I had a minimum three weeks immobilization in a sick bed, and this with three weeks to go before carnival! Bad timing indeed, but it was just as well that we were living in a pleasant house and not in some fleapit hotel. What could I do but make the best of it. I had plenty of time to delve through the fine collection of Brazilian popular music discs that our host Belen owned. Apart from the more well known artists such as Joao Gilberto, Jobim, Veloso and Gilberto Gil (who we had seen in concert a couple of weeks before) it was then that I got to listen to Vinicius, Ellis Regina, Beth Carvallho as well as the newer generation of musicians (back then in the early 80's) such as Gal Costa, Djavan, and Milton Nascimiento to name just a few. She also had a wide selection of folk music mostly in the Nord-Este style where songs with guitar and voice were usually accompanied by a deftly played pandeiro, triangle and other percussion. One of my favourite albums was a collection by the flute marching bands of Pernambuco: "Pifano do Norte", similar to the music we had heard in Lencois. Although Belem's record collection undoubtedly helped me while away the hours, I'll never know whether the remedy to my illness suggested by her condomble healer acquaintance was also effective. Modern medicine's only suggestion was rest and the consumption of large quantities of sugar in the form of a sweet Guava-based solidified jelly. The shaman recommended urinating over a particular stone heated by immersion in boiling water to which had been added a selection of medicinal plants. I tried both methods. Boredom was also alleviated by a thumb piano that I was travelling with, and at least I came away with some songs that I had composed. But one of my most vivid memories from this time was waking up one day to the chiming of bells from the local church – San Antonio. I could hardly believe it. In Salvador even church bells are played with a bossa rhythm!

Time went very slowly as I recuperated on my sick bed knowing that out in the streets the festivities were reaching their climax. In fact, though really too weak to move around much, so as not to feel I had missed all the fun I managed to stumble out of the house and around some local streets in the early hours of the final night of carnival. I don't remember what I was expecting, but in fact it was rather depressing. Apart from the occasional drunk or clinging pair of lovers, the only action on the nearly deserted streets was from the army of municipal workers clearing away the mounds of rubbish. This was the culmination of over two months revelling, and it was as if the population of Salvador had finally succumbed to a collective exhaustion. I still needed a few days before I was well enough to get around and see friends, but in fact our time in Bahia was coming to an end. We had been there for over three months but our budget was not limitless and there were areas of Brazil we still wanted to visit. In spite of my unfortunate illness, our time in Salvador had been unforgettable.

We said our sad farewells and took a coach through Pernambuco and then the scrub desert of North Eastern Brazil known as the Sertao, before arriving in Fortaleza, capital of the state of Ceara. From this region my strongest memories are of a family in a small fishing village called Almofala. Here there was poverty just around the corner for many families. The money we paid a fisherman to string up our hammocks in the front room, would most definitely help his family's precarious income. The several children they had were undernourished and basic medicines to alleviate simple yet painful problems were way beyond their means. Yet typical of the generosity we found in Brazil, the mother would go to the trouble of making meals that they would rarely have prepared for themselves. Imagine Esperanza and I tucking in to a delicious turtle stew with four or five hungry children hovering at the edge of the table with wide eyes on our plates. It was too much for us, and we would slip food to the kids and pay extra to the family. I got on well with the fisherman. He had built his own boat with his father, made the sail sewing together strips of material, and spent his spare time making his own fishing nets, as well as others that he would sell. One morning I went out with him on his boat, a sleek jangada, the traditional one or two man fishing boats of Ceara. They were built with an extremely shallow hull and very short keel, more like a raft than a normal sailing boat, and they would glide at high speed over the water's surface with the help of its enormous sail. We went out for just a morning, catching almost nothing, but at certain times of the year he would be away for four or five days, alone in the middle of the ocean with nothing but water bread and fruit to keep heart and soul together. He told me that he had actually been further from his village out on the sea than on land, and this a man who didn't know how to swim!

Esperanza and I travelled slowly along the north coast of Brazil, stopping for some days in the beautiful city Sao Luis, the capital of Maranhao, and the island of Alcantara full of remnants of its past history involving Dutch and British occupation before reverting again to its Portuguese masters.

"...the deck would be thick with colourful hammocks..."

Belem, the old port at the mouth of the Amazon was our next destination, and it was from here that we bought our passage on a small cargo vessel that plied its trade among the villages and small towns on its way up river, 3,000km to Manaus. As a cheap method of local passenger transport these boats were very popular, and at times the deck would be thick with colourful hammocks, with barely enough room to climb in and out. The composition of the population in northern Brazil was very different from that in Bahia. There were fewer people with African ancestry, and Indian and mestizo culture was prevalent, this of course being reflected in the music typical of the region. I had adopted an obvious tactic for finding out what local music might interest me, and would recommend it to any traveller. You simply hang around the music record shops which are of course easy to find as they inevitably have a speaker blaring music out on to the street. When you hear something that interests you, its there for you to buy, and if the shopkeeper insists on playing the Bee Gees, it is usually not too complicated to ask him to play something local. In this way I found some of my favourite Brazilian music. The style up here near the equator seemed to have more in common with calypso of the Caribbean, particularly the Soca of Trinidad. The songs had a faster lilting rhythm, invariably with a sax taking a leading role. The captain of our boat on the Amazon was most surprised when I played a tape I had just bought. It was by Pinduco, a Carimbó musician from Belem, popular with the locals, but hardly known outside the region. I still have his tape, and others by musicians such as Jackson de Pandeira, a classic of the north-eastern Forro style of music. When I play them now what memories they revive.

A river and region as impressive as the Amazon deserves a much more detailed description than this tale allows. I've come to the conclusion that there is another book to be written about our travelling adventures. There are so many memories of people and places when you start writing about travel experiences that there is not really place for them in this "musical" memoir. Let's just say we continued our way up this enormous artery through a vast region of rainforest twice the size of Europe containing two thirds of the planet's known plant species, astonished by a never ending series of events and sights. As for the people we met, there was of course almost the same level of diversity as in the local insect world. I was struck by the story of a young unemployed aircraft pilot from the south making his way to Manaus and a most uncertain future. Apparently there was a heavy demand for pilots to fly supplies into the numerous mining sites scattered over the region. Problem was that they would so overload the cargo that often the runway cut out of the forest just would not be long enough... Hence the scarcity of pilots!! We were made aware of the endemic hardship of the area on many occasions. When one mother with three or four young children in her charge discovered we were married but without children it was enough for her to beg us to take one of her children with us. Of course it would have been one less mouth to feed for her, and more food for the remaining kids.

A curious event occurred while on the banks of the River Tapajoz near the sleepy riverside town of Santarem. We were suddenly attacked by an army of stinging "fire" ants. Where else to retreat but in to the muddy waters of the river itself, and within minutes we had attracted the very close attentions of a school of Billabong, the strangely shaped Amazonian "sea" cow, some six feet long, who came gliding at full speed towards you, veering off just at the last minute. I had read somewhere that they were harmless, but...

Suffice it to say that finally we arrived at the unique city of Manaus, two million people squeezed into an island of "civilization" that had grown with the rubber boom and collapsed just as quickly after the Brits had stolen some rubber-tree seeds at the end of the 19th century and planted them in a much more organized fashion in Malaysia. Its famous opera house had been silent for years, but the city was now recovering fast as the maverick centre for the exploitation (and death?) of the vast resource-rich region surrounding it. Two thousand miles from the coast and without road connections - at least when we were there in the early 80's, it had a strange "frontier" atmosphere, a modern day gold-rush town. For a month we were guests of the kind family of a distant cousin of Esperanza who was involved in the collection of diamonds for the watch industry. We then travelled down to the

Bolivian border via coach, boat and a four-seater plane low over the jungle; eventually made our way through to La Paz; suffered altitude sickness before rowing out to the Island of the Moon on lake Titicaca; acquired a gold tooth from the local mines; narrowly missed gaol on the Bolivian/Brazilian border and finally made our way back to our friends in Rio for a final week's spree, spending the last cents of that Pil publishing money.

Chapter 16   Rainstorms and Dogg

Ten months after leaving we were back in London, and after visiting friends and family the first thing I wanted to do was to get back to playing. The possibility was offered by old friend and neighbour Gina, bass player with The Raincoats. Since I'd last played with them, the band had undergone various changes. In '78 with Vicky an accomplished violinist, Palmolive on drums and the original members Ana and Gina, they had recorded one of the classic discs of the time with Rough Trade. They'd followed this up with a second album "Odyshape" in 1980, with Charles Haywood replacing Palmolive and the collaboration of Robert Wyatt. Now, in the summer of '82 they were at another point of change, and finally the new group format settled down with the addition of Paddy on sax, Derek with the percussion and myself on drums.

We rehearsed at Vicky's place in Brixton, and started working on a new set of songs. I felt very much at home. Original ideas would be brought to the band room and what could be a prolonged process of editing, adding and arranging would eventually result in the finished songs. The very different styles of the people involved was for me a great strength within this procedure. Ana's approach was very personal. Her poems were snatched as if from a dream world then wrapped in a dissonance of melody and jangled, strident guitar chords. Gina on the other hand was more down to earth, but with a wit in her lyrics and a more classic approach to the melody and structure. With the addition of Vicky's musical skills both in playing and arranging, the set that we eventually worked up was a powerful mixture derived from our different musical influences and experiences. There was of course no direct conscious effort to copy any particular style, and I think we ended up with a sound very much our own. As drummer I felt free to experiment with whatever pattern I could come up with, and with the music encountered on our recent travels I was not short of inspiration on that score. To be working with Derek was another big plus. A real pleasure to be playing with him, as apart from him being one of my closest friends, we shared the same musical tastes and certainly clicked in the rhythm section. I also brought a couple of my songs in to the band room. One we worked up for the live set, the other eventually was included in the album.

In fact the offer of a gig with the new line-up came after just a couple of weeks of rehearsals, and we played our first set in Meanwhile Gardens as part of the Notting Hill carnival celebrations. The band had built up a reasonable following in the five years of its existence. It was not too hard to find gigs that were often part of the 'alternative' rock circuit. Shirley looked after the management side of things, and the whole set up functioned smoothly. Of course, we had to work very much on a shoe string as Rough Trade Records did not deal in big advances so there was only just enough to cover expenses. Surprisingly perhaps, given the disparate nature of the music, I think the band worked very well live, and we were to perform a number of memorable gigs. One in a small, upstairs dive in Glasgow, plus the usual round of London venues such as the Venue in Victoria or the U.L.U. in Malet Street. The lead vocals would be shared pretty much equally between Gina and Ana. Vicky, although mostly playing violin, would also pick up an occasional guitar and contribute to vocals, and Derek would take over from me on drums for two or three songs. For one of these changes I would pull out a Bolivian charango I had brought back from South America, and accompany the song I had written with the band. Paddy, apart from saxes and penny whistle, would also take over on bass on a couple of songs, so there would be quite a coming and going during the set. It really was a pleasure playing with the group. The fact that it was basically a women's band lent a very definite stamp to its identity, and although ego clashes and the normal personality problems did exist (and were to eventually explode!), if you can generalize, the overall mood was for me much more congenial than most all-male bands.

The press sometimes alluded to them as a "feminist" group, but I don't think they would have described themselves as that. It was true that, naturally enough, they had scant regard for the normal stereotyped image of women in society and particularly in rock. A number of their lyrics would treat with the subject of male /female relations in this male dominated society of ours, and of course the male sex did not necessarily come off in the best light (check out the lyrics of "Animal Rhapsody" from the album "Moving"), but generally I think their concerns were of a more "universal" nature.

Although the group was of course essentially Ana, Gina, and Vicki's, the day to day decisions made in the rehearsal room or when recording were taken by all of us, including the recent male additions. In fact I think that to an extent our presence acted as a balance to what increasingly was becoming a dichotomy in the musical direction of the band, with two distinct leanings - Gina and Vicki on one hand, Ana and Shirley on the other. Nothing very unusual in that, as every group has its internal balance of friendship, power, jealousy, or just musical tastes, but after six years the band was reaching a crucial point.

One of the greatest strengths of the band, its diversity, was starting to pull it apart. Hardly surprising really, as it's a scenario fraught with potential disaccord and problems. Another factor that came in to the equation was the relative lack of success of the band at the time. Despite being a firm favourite with both an unconditional fan base and a hard core of "alternative" music press journalists, since the first album there had been no real commercial success measured in terms of disc sales. They had been playing the scene for nearly six years, and particularly Gina and Vicki were itching to see more happening with the band. They wouldn't have wanted to become another "Bananarama", but they would have been more than happy to receive just a fraction of their recognition

However, these were problems that were to come to the surface as 1983 proceeded. For now there was studio time booked to start recording an album for Rough Trade, and we received a fillip with the arrival of Ernest Mogotse Mothle and his double-bass. From the first rehearsal that he came to in Brixton we were immediately bowled over by his presence, both personally and musically. He was one of several great South African musicians who had made their home in London and played the jazz circuit in Britain. I had seen Ernie play with his compatriot the sax player Dudu Pakwana, but Ernie had done the rounds of numerous jazz formations. He was a fantastic player, and we selected three songs that we preferred to record with the warmth of his acoustic double bass.

The album was to be recorded at various London studios over the next few months, but to start with we went in to Regent Park Studios with Adam Kidron at the controls. I remember there being a fair bit of confusion as to who decided what in terms of the production, with for example Adam's idea for the inclusion of a horn section and a bass synth for "Anima Rhapsody" not receiving unanimous approval, but overall things went pretty smoothly. We laid down some good tracks, Ernie playing on the fine track "Overheard", and a song of mine "Dreaming in the Past" with Derek adding a lovely waltz beat on drums. Despite the ever wider gap between the approach of Gina and that of Ana, discussion would usually solve the problem and result in a compromise solution. Vicky's violin was for me essential to the sound of the band, as of course were the soaring harmonized vocals which had been a fundamental part of this sound from the band's inception. The saxes and penny whistle of Paddy were a new element within the instrumentation, and in my opinion sat well in the finished mixes.

At the beginning of December we had confirmation of a mini tour of New England. Ruth Polsky in New York not only acted as our agent, she also arranged for us to stay in the flats of friends and did a fine job looking after her charges. It was all pretty low budget, but in fact much more enjoyable to be staying in the room of someone's apartment than in some downbeat hotel...... We arrived in a New York under two foot of snow, but were immediately impressed by the kindness of Ruth and her friends. We were all staying down on the lower East side, around an alphabet city still to be yuppified in the early 80's, and so with a high proportion of junkies and general street corner hang-abouts.

I fell in love with New York from this first visit. I found the people so open and friendly, and if I had thought London cosmopolitan, well NYC was something else.

Raincoats, Pyramid Club, NYC

Derek and I were pretty much inseparable, and we padded the streets and marvelled at the different Manhattan neighbourhoods, from Russian, Polish, Jamaican, Puerto Rican, Cuban, up to black Harlem back down to Jewish Brooklyn. We sought out music clubs and were thrilled to meet personally the great jazz drummer and vibe legend Lionel Hampton, even if it was just a few words and a shake of his hand.

The first gig we had was at the trendy "Danceteria" club, which was booking a lot of the current British post – punk bands. It was a good gig and we went down well with the crowd. I remember John Lydon being there. He had always been very enthusiastic about the band, and here was no exception. We had some wild times: there was always something going on through the night, but what was to turn out to be the most enjoyable gig of the tour for me was an off-the-cuff offer to play a small club in our neighbourhood: the Pyramid on Avenue A. It wasn't till two or three in the morning that we played, a hilarious Drag show having opened the show. It was a transvestite club, full of extremely glamorous man-ladies. They loved our music, and I remember we seemed to play for hours. I have always preferred to play in small clubs, with the closeness of the audience to the stage and the intimate atmosphere being obviously the important factor, and this was one of those gigs.

The rest of our dates were out of town, and we piled in to a van and headed off down to Philadelphia and Washington. Nothing very special there and we came back to NYC with a few days before the return flights and very little money in our pockets. I can't remember whether Neil Cooper at Noir records organized the gig at the Kitchen, but their suggestion to record the concert there was opportune. The Kitchen was a Performing Arts club down in Soho, and not really the best venue for a live recording. The vibe at the Drag club we had played a few days before was a hundred times hotter than the rather serious arty audience that turned up to the show, expecting perhaps some high brow conceptual art performance. However, they did in fact warm up by the end, the gig was not that bad, and the extra dollars from the record company allowed us to enjoy our last few days in the city and come home with some spare cash.

Back in London we went straight in to recording, this time at Berry Street Studios. I can't remember exactly but I think the recording process was spread over a couple of months ... sessions being organized as money became available. Listening to the album now, I am surprised at the level of cohesion that was actually achieved. Apart from the songs "Avidoso" that I sang and was happy to get Richard Summers to play trumpet on, and "Animal Rhapsody" , the rest of the album moves easily between the songs sung by Gina or Ana. Ana's more austere "Mouth of a Story" or "Balloon" blend with Vicky's highlife guitar on "Honey Mad Woman", and then to Gina's funk inspired "Dance of Hopping Mad" which we recorded down at Olympic Studios in Barnes. One of my favourites tracks was "Rainstorm" written and sung by Gina. A slow moody beginning picked up into a fast swinging groove with Ernie holding down a soaring line on the double bass.

Rainstorm on the Thames...

Talking of which, it was because of this song that saw us heading off one blustery afternoon to the vicinity of Hammersmith Bridge. We hired a rowing boat and I was unpleasantly surprised at the strong pull of the Thames current. Gina had decided to set the action for a "Rainstorm" 16mm short film on the river, and having volunteered to take the oars I ended up soaked to the skin and with blisters on my hands. An island in the middle of the Thames was to be an essential shot, and on attempting to disembark there we nearly ended up with a capsized boat and more than wet feet. Aptly enough it was pouring with rain, and we eventually arrived back on dry land, a bedraggled bunch needing blankets and shots of brandy, convinced that the world of the silver screen was for hardier souls.

All in all I think it was a very special album that we finally produced, and it faithfully reflected the band's position at the time as one of the more interesting post-punk entities. However, as '83 progressed the rifts within the band that I have already mentioned came more and more to the surface. I suppose a culminating point was when it was decided to bring out a 12 inch single. At the time Chrysalis were showing some interest in sorting out a publishing deal, and this fact no doubt influenced the choice of what was considered the more commercial "Animal Rhapsody" with its dance rhythms, funky bass synth, and papping horn section. It was miles away from Ana's more introspective often dark and dissonant music, and the sessions we did with Dennis Bovell at the controls, were some of the last we did together as a group. The more "pop" oriented approach espoused by Gina and Vicky were stretching far from Ana's natural ground, and within a few weeks the band was no more. Gina and Vicky were to work together in a mid 80's "dance" project called "Dorothy", and I played a gig or two with Gina in Mayo Thompson's "Red Crayola", but the Raincoats weren't to reappear until the mid 90's, when Kurt Cobain sought out Ana and instigated a Raincoats renaissance.

The happy memories that I had of working with the band were somewhat soured when I read a version of the band's '83 demise that later came out in print. Kurt Cobain's appreciation of the first Raincoats album led to a reforming of the band in '96 with the emphasis that Ana gave to the band very much to the fore. Good luck to them I thought at the time, but to my chagrin I would later see an article in which the blame for the '83 break-up is laid at the door of the "drummer they had got in", where the fact that I wrote a song or two, made things go "strange"! It seems as if in '96 it was deemed important for Ana and Gina to project an image of unity and continuity, conveniently forgetting the differences they'd had 13 years before, and creating yours truly as the fall guy! Therefore, it was no real surprise when, with the re-release of the Moving album as a CD on Geffen, publishing credits and payments were conveniently forgotten for certain quarters, despite the existence of previous contracts that defined the situation quite clearly. Oh well, the re-writing of history has followed me around this tale on enough occasions for me not to worry unduly about it!

*

Towards the end of '83 with things going strange in the Raincoats department I had hooked up again with my old mate Tymon Dogg. His latest album "Battle of Wills" had just been released on Y - Records, and that project was the result of a series of memorable events that he had organized at the Enterprise pub in Chalk Farm a couple of years previously. At those gigs I would sometimes share percussion duties with Chic McLaughlin who was to play on the album, and Helen Cherry would share vocals with Dogg. Helen had an extraordinary voice and stage presence, and I was honoured when she offered to sing a song I had penned, and would later be covered by The Raincoats: "Dreaming in the Past", writen to the memory of my dear sister Elizabeth who had recently comitted suicide in most distraught circumstances.

When the Raincoats finally ground to a halt, Tymon and I decided to look for a bassist, and we were lucky to have Ralf Schmidt, a German musician, living in the same house as me in Monmouth Road. Within a few weeks we were gigging as a trio. The style of things wasn't that different from 1977 when we had started "The Fools", although Dogg's irrepressible creativity had of course given rise to a whole bunch of new songs. The same blistering lyrics and passionate delivery were still in place and we played a number of concerts in and around London during the following months.

Since the "Fools" days back in '77 and '78, Tymon had been playing with innumerable musicians and a variety of projects, but in general he remained a solo performer with violin and voice, usually playing small venues though I do remember one gig he had supporting The Pretenders at Hammersmith Odeon. On a tour of U.S. clubs in 1980 (with Mickey Foote helping out on the sound) he had met up with the Clash in New York. They were recording the epic Sandinista! album at Electric Lady, and Tymon got involved on a number of tracks with his violin, as well as recording one of his songs "Lose this Skin" that was later included on the album. This was the first time that Tymon and Joe had played together since the 101'ers gigs at the Elgin, and it led to more collaborations on the following Clash album "Combat Rock", but despite these reunions it came as a very pleasant shock when Joe contacted Tymon with the suggestion of producing an album of his songs.

When Joe had had problems with the mixing of "Combat Rock" he had turned to Glyn Johns to help out. If ever there was a mythical figure in British rock music studio work, Glyn was the man, with his experience during the 60's and 70's working with just about everyone including the Beatles, Stones, Led Zep, the Who etc etc.... So, we were well chuffed at Joe's suggestion of doing the recordings with him. For the next couple of weeks we would pile in to my beaten up red Morris Minor Post Office van and trundle down to the studio at Glyn's Sussex home, my "Noddy" vehicle standing somewhat incongruously next to the E-types and what have you parked in the paddock. The recording was done in a very relaxed manner, and Glyn John's method of recording in as "live" a way as possible suited Tymon's material to a "T". I was a big fan of this approach. Click tracks for drummers, and 20 microphones spread around a drum kit were not my idea for the best way of capturing music, and Glyn was very much of the school of recording engineers that liked to keep things simple. I think there were no more than six mikes on the kit, and another facet of the sessions was the relatively low number of takes that we would do. Maximum of three for the rhythm tracks, and we had a dozen songs down in three or four days. Tymon played all the other instruments - piano, Spanish guitar, electric and acoustic guitar, viola and violin and the vocal parts.

Joe didn't miss a session, and although the final mix decisions were left to Glyn and Tymon (often not without a fiery discussion) he was always there with suggestions and with his unquenchable enthusiasm. We had a great time those few weeks. With Joe and Tymon I had always felt not just the highest regard as musicians, but also a close affinity as friends. I think Joe at that time was under severe pressure over the state of affairs in the Clash, and hopefully he found some relatively light relief in the project. We'd often stop off at a pub on the way back to London and whether it was a guffaw over our latest antics that day in the studio, or a shared reminiscence from our squatting days in Maida Hill, I have the memory now of drifting back in to London as if from a child's dream world. Probably the effect of the Shepherd Neam best bitter.

Some fine tracks came out of the session. A haunting "Velvet Stella" with Tymon on piano and Ralf on double bass is my favourite; "Moth in to a Flame", "Scrape of a Deal", "Hollowed Out" were other great recordings, and there were enough songs for an album which was of course the next stage in the operation. Having paid for all the studio time, Joe didn't think twice about funding a return ticket to N.Y.C. so that I could punt the songs around some publishing houses and record companies. If there was someone who put his money where his mouth was it was Joe Strummer. In all my dealings with him over the years, I don't think money was ever a motivation for him. Fame yes ... but not fortune.

There was some vague interest in the songs I was touting around, but no one in the biz that I contacted saw any commercial potential in the recordings, and since then the material has remained more or less parked on a shelf... In fact in 2002, a month before Joe died, the multi-track tapes were stacked up in the porch of Joe's house down in Somerset. He'd left them there with the intention of resurrecting the music almost 20 years after the recordings had been made. One day, I'm sure, the music will see the light of day.

Tymon, Ralf and I carried on playing live through '84 and '85. We had a couple more recording sessions, one with Mike Finesilver at the controls in the EMI Manchester Square studios. With the possibilities of a publishing deal for Tymon, the production was maybe aiming at a sound that didn't really sit well with Tymon's music. He was later to home produce a much more interesting set of songs that he eventually released on his own label as the album titled "Relentless".

With Ralf moving back to Germany and then to Australia, the project stumbled to a halt, and it would be another 18 years before I shared a stage with Tymon again. Meanwhile, I had decided on a course of action that would drastically change my circumstances.

Chapter 17 Decomposition

My soft spot for things Hispanic went beyond the fact that I had a Spanish wife. Since my first time in Spain back in 1974, I had retained at the back of my mind the idea that one day I'd like to live there and so I had asked Fernando, Esperanza's brother living in Granada, to keep an eye out for any cheap, dilapidated property; dilapidated because of course we couldn't dream of affording anything pricey. Esp had five thousand pounds in an account in Spain so that was our budget, and even back then it was a small amount of cash to buy a house! Granada had always appealed to me as a possible place to live. The slumbering Alhambra, overlooking a city steeped in history with a crumbling yet lived-in old quarter. The fact that it was a university town with sixty thousand students kept its spirit young, and it had/has an active cultural life in which music forms an important part.

As in all Andalusia, Flamenco music is very much a living folk genre, and in Granada the large gypsy population ensures the tradition is maintained. Though by no means exclusively a Gypsy music, there is no doubt in my mind that the Gitanos are the prime force within the music, and what a music it is. The "Blues of Europe" Robert Wyatt called it. Stunningly powerful rhythms, incredible virtuosity on the guitar, and soulful, plaintive vocals. At the same time Granada had a reputation, going back to the 60's, for producing rock and roll, so all in all it wasn't as if our projected move would be a complete adios to music. What was furthest from our mind was to "retire" either to some British expat enclave on the coast, or bury ourselves in a small Spanish village in the countryside. What I loved about the character of Spanish society was its vibrancy and openness, and Granada seemed the ideal place, neither too big nor too small, to which to make the move. One morning we received a letter from Fernando with some very interesting photos and I went straight out to the nearest travel agent to book a plane ticket to Andalusia and check out the ruin he had found.

Esperanza and I had been over on a couple of previous occasions to see some places, but this time Fernando had came up trumps with something very special. Perched on a hill backing on to the Alhambra woods, overlooking the city centre which was just five minutes away, the house was pretty much derelict, and in a neighbourhood that had been abandoned for years. Perfect, the price was right and we would be able to renovate it in our own manner and at our own pace. We bought the place without hesitation, but of course all this would have important repercussions, as it was a project that was going to need funding far beyond the cash figures that we were used to.

We had been existing for years on a day to day basis without any regular income. Esperanza had finished her degree at Camberwell School of Art and had then been admitted to a postgraduate course in ceramics at the Royal College of Art. Having finished there in 1985, she had set up her own workshop and was now having considerable success, working full time on commissions and for exhibitions in specialist London galleries. But even so, the activity was no great money winner. The same with myself. Income from music was precarious to say the least. I had decided long ago that I did not want to work as a session musician, and unfortunately for my bank account, I was very choosy when it came to working with other musicians.

I had consequently been involved in all manner of scams other than music to scrape a living yet maintain control over the hours I worked, and thus allow myself time for whatever musical project I fancied. At around this period I was involved in a distinctly shady "cowboy" operation: "Bayswater Builders". My comrade-in-arms and friend Simon Bramley knew as much (or as little) as I did about building, but we had to learn fast as a few ads placed in local papers and shops resulted in a demand for our services. Painting and decorating extended to some more serious building and plumbing jobs, which truth be told were well beyond our abilities! We got in to all manner of escapades, but usually managed to somehow squirm our way out of them, and had an enjoyable time on the way.

Another operation that I embarked on involved flogging ceramics that were produced in a small pottery in Stoke-on-Trent on the brink of closing that my father had recently taken on as a favour to the widowed owner. The fact that I could help out my Dad, albeit in a small way, was an additional plus to the venture. I lined the inside of an old suitcase with black velvet, arranged a selection of ceramic animals and Beefeater jugs within it, polished my shoes, and traipsed the streets of London's West End searching out gift shops that would put in an order. In fact several of them did, but unfortunately there were few re-orders.

As for my music, almost all the projects I got involved in were financial no-goers, and the new one that I started after being with Tymon was no exception. I had first worked with Jim the Bass, (alias Amos, alias L'Voag, alias Xentos, alias Harmon e. Phraisyar etc) in the "NoName" band after my stint with Pil, and had remained in contact since then. Everything Jim touched he converted in to something special. He made many recordings, all coming to light on DIY pressings (I hesitate at calling it "his own label"), which would change name from project to project, as would his own personal moniker. This was just yet one more rejection on his behalf of the normal code of commercial practice. It was as if he stalked a subterranean musical twilight zone, with not just indifference to, but more like a positive loathing of, the surrounding rock/pop music world. It led him, in my opinion, to create some of the zaniest music around at the time, and the great thing was that it seemed as if it were all perfectly natural for him. He oozed talent, yet was absolutely out of the main stream and his irreverent sense of humour would balance out what could be a heavy dose of blackness... A poseur he was not, and neither would his keen musical sense allow him to get bogged down in the navel gazing antics as it did, for example, with so many free-form jazzers. You can see I'm a very big fan of his, and I did not need any encouragement to join forces with him again.

He was now playing keyboards with a hot bass player - Ron, and after a few sessions we were also joined by old School House cohort Lepke Buchwater coming in on guitar. The music encompassed many rhythmic styles: ranging through hard funky, bossa, or reggae to a manic rock, usually with a strong improvised element. Within this structure, underpinned by Ron's funked out bass, Jim would weave his strident keyboard chords/noises, occasional trumpet and singular voice. Apart from Lepke other musicians would appear on a casual basis. To start with most of the rehearsals were in my basement flat in Monmouth Rd, and Jim came up with the perfect name - "The Decomposers".

concrete jungle fauna...

We found a venue for the first gig through our old friend Simon "Big John" Cassell. He had been involved in filming and acting in various "shorts" , and one day told me of an exciting "site" that he had stumbled on. I of course knew of the existence of a private hospital run by Spanish sisters literally 400yds away in the street parallel to ours near to Bayswater Road, but I hadn't noticed that it had ceased functioning as a hospital, presumably just a short time before. I went round there with Simon the following day and could hardly believe it. Simon changed the padlock on the front gate, and we walked in to a place that had obviously been recently abandoned yet amazingly with the electricity supply still connected. Not only that, but some of the equipment was still in evidence: beds, oxygen bottles and masks, drip-stands, even nurse's white coats and stethoscopes! Simon's interest in the place was as a ready-made set for a 16mm film that he wanted to shoot. I immediately saw the potential as a venue for our first gig, with a large meeting hall on the first floor. It was obvious that we would have to move fast. It appeared as if no one else had yet stumbled on Simon's discovery, and a large unoccupied hospital in Bayswater, still with its electricity supply, wouldn't remain unnoticed for long!

Simon didn't need telling that it would be a fantastic place for a gig, and of course I agreed with his suggestion that first they should finish the filming project that he had in mind. A concert, with the noise it would generate, would almost certainly attract the neighbours' attention, and on top of that it was just a few minutes from Kensington Palace Gardens, or Millionaire's Row as we knew it, packed solid with embassies and their accompanying police presence. It was likely that its life as a squat would be short lived.

We set the gig date for the following Saturday, and I started organizing things. We had to be careful with our publicity, not wanting to attract attention from the boys in blue, so we decided on word of mouth with sheets to be distributed around the Portobello/Notting Hill area on the day of the gig itself. Dubbed the "Hospital Happening", we had one group who wanted to play - a jazz band with Michelle from Si's house in Daventry Street, but there wasn't much time for finding another attraction. Then out of the blue I had a call from a friend from Malaga. Enrique was a teacher, and just happened to be over for a few days, looking after a gaggle of twenty or so Spanish teenage girls on holiday in London. I met them at their hotel and it was easy to persuade them to agree to put on a Flamenco dance show for us at the Happening. I had a few Flamenco tapes which I left with them so that they could get on with some practice, and they seemed as thrilled with the idea as I was. The night was shaping up with the promise of being a truly bizarre event, and we weren't to be disappointed. We got in there at eight in the evening and built a provisional stage with tea chests covered with chip-board. I didn't want the hassle of charging at the door, so instead we bought as many cans of beer as our finances would allow, and set up a rudimentary bar at the side of the stage, from where we could sell the cans and make a few bob. If the law was to make an appearance, we didn't want a possible problem because of the illegal selling of booze, so it was organized stealthily, all the cans being stashed in the tea chests covered by portions of the stage.

Our softly, softly publicity campaign had worked. People just kept turning up, and by ten o'clock it was pretty well packed out. The jazz band played, the flamenco girls danced, and we were just about to hit the stage around midnight, with Jim's taped sounds at full blast, when the Old Bill suddenly appeared at the back of the hall. Probably called up by some neighbours I feared the worse as I ambled over to a senior looking officer who was asking to speak to the person in charge:

- "Yes officer, of course we'll keep the sound level down..... yes officer, its just a temporary arrangement...... for sure officer, we'll be out of here by three in the morning......".

I could hardly believe it. He just turned around and led his men out the way he had come in. We turned the sound level down for a few minutes until we reckoned that they had left the premises, yanked the dial back up again, and got up to do our set. We had a great time. Inigo, the sax player who had played with The Vincent Units and Tesco Bombers, joined us with his alto, and a girl whose name I can't remember but was seriously out of her head added vocals and a form of dancing.... All in perfect keeping with a truly surreal night. In the early hours, we loaded up the van with gear and stage, and left never to return.

*

Prior to this first gig, with the house project in Granada obviously going to need a serious injection of cash over the next couple of years, I had received a timely offer from my old friend Ian Walley. He needed help with the general organization of his stage lighting company - Avolites, and I agreed to work for him on a full time basis for two years, the first job requiring such a commitment since I had started playing music. To start with I was pretty despondent, feeling that finally I had succumbed to the pressure of having a full time job outside music, but I quickly got involved with what was a hefty challenge. Of course, initially I knew nothing of management, health & safety regs, staff procurement procedures, production flow charts or strategic sales planning, but I had to learn damn fast, as we more or less re-structured the company, preparing it for the eventual sale that was Ian's ultimate goal. Besides, my involvement with "The Decomposers" didn't let up as we moved our rehearsal studio to Jim's place in Shepherd's Bush, did some recording on his 4-track and started looking for gigs.

As a result of the income from Avolites, I was able to get over to Granada every six months or so, and organize work on the house. It really was a wreck: worse than any of the squats we had repaired back in Maida Hill, and for the first few visits my brother and sister-in-law, Fernando and Mariela, would kindly put us up at their place, while we tore our house apart. Over the next three years we had invaluable help from friends. Jim, Simon Bramley, Little Richard, Kate and Graham, as well as my brothers and Dad who all came over at different times and lent a hand wherever they could. The basic deal was that we would pay for the flights and all their expenses, and they would help with the general labouring or whatever they could do. Apart from this help we of course employed a local bricklayer and his mate and I would buy the materials and generally organize the site. It was in fact very enjoyable. Hard work during the day, and hard play at night when we would invariably make our way to the lively Granada bars. It was a heavy schedule, burning the candle at both ends, with the daily grind mixing cement and what-have-you, but it was quite an experience. A lot of the work we did during the summer months, so that was another factor that had to be dealt with, as the temperatures would regularly soar well over 100ºF during the day.

The bricklayer and his muscular helper were an interesting pair of local characters. The mate, Manolo "Manogrande" (Big Hands), would have to return to prison every night after his day's labour. He was coming to the end of a prison sentence for murder, and was allowed out on parole during the day. In fact he was an honourable soul who I trusted more than the majority of other local contractors and merchants with whom I was dealing. One day he explained what had happened. He was nineteen years old, dancing in a club with a girl. The girl's "friend" appears. An argument starts, they pull their knives (they all used to carry knives), the bloke comes for him and ends up on the floor in a pool of blood and dies. I suspect there was mostly truth in the story as the judge only gave him nine years.

"... all the building materials ... would have to be brought up by donkey..."

As the house was situated up what could best be described as a goat track, all the building materials (sand, bricks and cement) would have to be brought up by donkey, or if not, on our sweaty backs. Regularly the donkeys wouldn't be there when they should have been, and I'd have to go off and scour the alleys of the old quarter looking for "Dog Killer", their owner. There were no architect's plans - just the advice of a surveyor friend, so in time-worn Spanish fashion, we did the work and paid a nominal fine to the Town Hall when the work was finished. Of course all this required that I learnt Spanish in double quick time, picking up on the way a very strong Granadino accent from my labouring mates.

By Spring 1988 the house in Granada was more or less finished, my time with Avolites was over, and the band too had decomposed after death by natural causes. It was time for the big move. We packed our things into a lorry, including the contents of Esp's ceramic studio, kiln and all, and hired a stall on Portobello from where we sold off our unwanted gear. We organized a party in the Tabernacle community centre to say our goodbyes and that was it, the end of fourteen very eventful years living in our London neighbourhood. In fact our final exit from Monmouth Road was undertaken in certain style. On returning to her native land Esperanza was allowed to import in to Spain, tax free, a car in her name, and so I had previously bought an old left hand drive black Porsche Targa 911 for this purpose, hoping that I could sell it in Spain at a good profit. So that's how we left Westbourne Grove, skimming through France and northern Spain in a top-less Porsche down to Madrid. There our dear friend Angel went to a safe in the wall, pulled out wads and wads of pesetas for us, and shooed us of to Granada in what would now be his Porsche once we had sorted out the papers. And so we arrived in Granada with enough cash in our pockets to see us through the first six months. But that wasn't all we had in our pouches. Esperanza had a little bundle inside, who would be born that Autumn and be called Luna. So yes, this really was a year of change.

Chapter 18 Spain Again

I knew that on coming to live in Spain major changes would be around the corner. If living from music had been hard for me in London, landing in Granada and starting a family would make it even more so. I was lucky, though, with the work I found, and within a few months was working as manager for an imaginative Granadino theatre group, "Etcetera". Speaking English helped with the many foreign tours that we organized, and I suppose my background was relevant to the theatre milieu in which they moved. On leaving them after three years or so, I continued in the world of production, which is my prime occupation to this date. Classical music festivals; jazz festivals;   live cultural TV programmes; cultural TV documentaries in Spain, Morocco and Portugal; documentaries for the BBC, and Discovery; rock concerts ..... you name it, and despite Granada being a relatively small city, I just about keep things afloat. I suppose this type of work suits my personality. You work intensely with a team for a few days or weeks, or at most a couple of months, and then the project is finished. Everyone leaves and I'll be looking for the next one. It's such varied work that I certainly don't have time to get bored.

Two recent projects I researched and produced for Japanese channel NHK, with our friend Yuko, were particularly interesting. One on vocal music in the Iberian peninsula, encompassing Flamenco, Fado, and Spain's rich choral tradition; the other, a return to the squatting world that I had known so many years previously. But what a tragic return. The phenomenon that I was researching was not the young-person's alternative society version of which I had been a part in London, but rather the knock-on effect of the current Spanish economic crisis. A generation (part of the 25% unemployed), in their late middle age, and from one day to the next left without work and soon out on the street being unable to keep up the mortgage payments. Courageous, "ordinary" people suddenly thrust in to the role of urban guerrillas fighting for survival.

Por Si Las Moscas.....Granada, 1994
Ester, Juanma, R, Eva, Carlos & Ramon

As to music, within a couple of years after our move down to Granada, I was back again in the process of forming a band. We called ourselves "Por Si Las Moscas", which translates in meaning, if not literally, as "just in case". With a two girl vocal chorus and sax, apart from lead and rhythm guitar, it was a good time dance band, and we were able to rehearse in a backroom on the ground floor of our house. We wrote the songs either collectively or from the pen of Ramon, the singer. We had no problem finding gigs, whether as support for known bands or in the many small venues that Granada had at the time. Our friend Angel, owned a recording studio as well as a lighting and sound equipment company in Madrid, so we eagerly took up his offer to record there. At around this time I was talking to Joe on the phone and I mentioned the fact that I was recording with my new band. He offered to lend a hand with the mixing, and in fact came over when we were still putting down the final voice tracks, and stayed on till the album was finished. As with Tymon's Glyn Johns album, he wouldn't hear of taking any payment for his work, or the hotel or flights, and always insisted on paying for the drinks when we hit the town at night. The album was released on a local Granada label, and although the band folded within six months around '95, we did have the pleasure of launching the disc in an original manner. We received sponsorship from the local "Alhambra" beer company and were able to use their lorry, kitted out with a portable generator, to tour the city, playing for hours from the back of the truck.

When the band folded I carried on playing for a time with a Moroccan group "Al Jaima". I enjoyed it especially for the challenge of new rhythms that I had to learn, but soon launched a new enterprise when hooking up with a British sound engineer recently arrived in Granada with the equipment to set up a recording studio, but no premises in which to install it. We remodelled the ground floor of our house, and from there ran a commercial studio. The most interesting production that we organized was with a group of young kids called "Taller de Compás". Through the dedication of their monitor, Puche, a flamenco percussion and singing group resulted from a housing project centred in the most marginalized of Granada's slum areas. It helped keep young Gypsy kids off the streets, giving them the possibility of continuing with a career in music. There were two groups, one with kids from ages six to twelve, and another for those that had progressed from the younger group and were able to perform live gigs. We recorded an album for them, before another recording session of note which was for the first album by local cantaora Estrella Morente, with her father Enrique overseeing the production. It was an honour for us to have the great Pepe Habichuela in to put down the flamenco guitar tracks. Finally my partnership with the engineer soured, and we called it a day.

My next project started in the autumn of 2002, when I was at a party in which a band was playing in the back room. My ears pricked up as I heard the strains of a manic blue grass version of "You Really Got Me". I liked what I heard, and was very impressed with the singing and strumming on an electrified acoustic by the band's lead singer, so during the break asked if I could join them on percussion of some kind as they didn't have a drummer. That was the start of an association with New Jersey songster/strummer Tom Lardner, which has lasted till the present. I did a couple of rehearsals with them, and what had been "The Country Dogs" became "The Dogs of Paradise" and we started to look for gigs in the New Year.

However, in December, a sad event occurred which was to crucially effect the development of the group: Joe Strummer died.

*

From the mid 80's and the demise of the Clash Joe had been coming regularly to Spain, following up an interest in its culture that had started back in the 101'ers days. Via the discs of Paco Ibañez, Paloma and Esperanza had introduced him to the poetry of Federico Garcia Lorca, the Granadine poet shot at the start of the Spanish civil war, and also to flamenco music which I know became a firm favourite with him.

Apart from that, though, I think Joe's nature simply clicked with the Spanish life style: its openness, its street life, the passion , and importantly, its nocturnal bias. Having had the initial contact with Esperanza's brother Fernando, he quickly got to know the Granada night scene and local musicians, which was to lead to him producing an album for the Granada rock band "091" in 1986. In the same year he also became involved in the filming of Alex Cox's "Straight to Hell", shot in the desert wastelands around Tabernas, Almeria; an area in Southern Spain that had been used in the 60's for the filming of various "spaghetti westerns" amongst other film productions. On the coast close by, within the Natural Park of Cabo de Gata, he stumbled on what was then the relatively small and sleepy village of San Jose. He would return here at least once a year from then on, it becoming a kind of summer retreat for him, and this lead to us meeting up most years if only for a few days.

Tymon Dogg had also made a strong connection with Granada, actually coming to live with his family for extended periods during the mid/late 90's. In fact, we had recorded together in Granada on a song for an album that I was producing in 1998 to commemorate Federico Garcia Lorca's centenary. The track was by Granada rock band Lagartija Nick, which we recorded in the studio of the great afore mentioned flamenco singer Enrique Morente. I had contacted Tymon to suggest his collaboration with voice and violin on the song based on a Lorca poem. My contribution was limited to just a few bars played on a Santoor, the beautiful hammer-dulcimer type instrument, one of which I had bought whilst on a working trip in Iran. Shortly after that recording I was very happy to learn that Tymon and Joe had linked up in the new band that Joe had recently formed - "The Mescaleros". They had met at a sad occasion in early '99: a get together in Notting Hill to pay tribute to Mole, the 101'ers bass player who had recently died. It was the first time that Joe and Tymon had played together on stage since the Elgin 101'ers gigs back in 1975.

I was also to link up with Joe on stage, albeit just for one song, again with a twenty five year time span since our Soul Vendor gigs in the Tabernacle. The Mescaleros were playing the Cambridge Folk Festival in early August 2002. I just happened to be over in the UK and I arrived at the festival site with Esperanza and our two teenagers Luna and Giggs as the heavens opened in a torrential downpour just before their set. I saw Joe as they were heading on stage, and he screamed out to me "Nº6, come on for Nº6!" .Sure enough, I grabbed a tambourine or something, and played along with my old mates Tymon and Joe, but it was what happened after the gig that I remember most vividly. Joe couldn't do enough for us. With all the post gig hassles that he had to handle, including press interviews and the like, he insisted that we join them on the tour bus. Looking after Esp who wasn't too well, making sure the kids were ok, listening with them to the music they were playing on their disc players, getting me to respond to the journalist, it was all just typical Joe.

Later that August we were to meet up again in San Jose. This time it was his 50th birthday, so big fiesta time. We started off at Pepe's Camping bar, and progressed to biker Jo's Bar in nearby Escullos.

All night birthday party....Cabo de Gata...

A party that went on, as ever with Joe, till sunrise. The following night was a full moon and we arranged to meet at midnight on one of the nearby coves. Esperanza and I were already there when a large group of Joe's family and friends eventually arrived. Joe went into "camping" mode, bringing out the bongos, the booze, blankets and all the necessaries, and again the session was to last till the light of dawn. The next morning we had to head back to Granada, and on the way out of the village we bumped into Joe at the entrance to a café. The last image I have of him is helping carry out the rubbish sacks from the bar. I was to speak with him a couple of days later on the phone. During the previous night's full-moon session by the sea, Joe had been talking at length about his current situation with the Meskies and music in general, and several times he had said how much it meant to him having Tymon on board, how important a collaborator he was, and how he couldn't see it working for long with the other guys, etc etc.. Of course there had been a lot of alcohol consumed and it could well have been just a phase, but I was left with such a strong impression that I felt I had to make clear one thing to him. If he were to ever arrive at the situation of being on his own with just Tymon, there was a drummer here that would like nothing more than to...

Who knows what would have happened, but a call from my brother Pat on the 22nd of December of that year gave us the news of his sudden death. I have thought since then of my reaction to the news, and tried to explain to myself the reasons for the inordinate depth of grief that I felt. Was it influenced in some strange way by the fame he had achieved? Was my disconsolate reaction somehow amplified by the same mechanism, the media hype, that helps create fame in the first place? In other words would my sadness have been the same if he had been a Joe public, an old friend who I had once shared good times with, but who I had not really had that much to do with in the previous twenty six years? Of course I will never know the answer to that one, but I think the most shocking aspect of Joe's death was the realization that a person with such an incredible zest for life and interest in people and ideas was suddenly, in a snap of the fingers, no longer there.

It was with a very heavy heart that I took a plane over to London for his funeral. Where else but back to the Harrow Road, just past Ladbroke Grove in our old neck of the woods, with an inevitable drizzle to accompany us. Luce his widow knew that here in this down-at-heel corner of west London was where Joe would have wished to say his last goodbyes. So many faces I knew or half knew at the pub after the service, but with Mickey, Derek and Tymon we drank a pint or three to the memory of our old mate. At one point there were Rat Scabies, Terry Chimes, Derek and myself having a chat together, and it had to be Mickey with a "What's this, a bleedin' drummers' convention!?", followed by a wry quip from Mick: "Yea, he always got on with you drummers best….".

*

Derek and I ended up that night in the bowels of Mickey's barge on the Grand Union Canal, just around the corner from the Kensal Green cemetery. It was the same freezing murky water lapping its bows that Joe had jumped into to save a drowning man twenty seven years before. The three of us decided there and then to set up some sort of get together to pay tribute to our friend. From the start I was clear in my mind as to the kind of tribute I wanted to organize. It would be local, low key and involve people from that time around '75 before Joe had become a rock icon, and it was obvious that a Joe-less 101'ers would have to perform. First of all I had to get the agreement of Clive and Dan. No problem. Both were still playing music and more than happy to participate. The problem was who was going to sing? Of course, my mate Tom back in Granada with who I had recently started playing would be perfect, with an attitude and style not so dissimilar from Joe, and certainly with a passion in his delivery that had reminded me of Joe the first time I had seen Tom play. The next thing to decide was the venue. Where better than the Tabernacle in Powis Square, just off Portobello Rd. The same ex-synagogue community centre that I had played with Joe in the Soul Vendors, with Tymon in the "Fools", with the Raincoats, and where Esp and I had celebrated our "adios" party on leaving Blighty.

As for the other acts, Tymon Dogg was a must, and I was dead keen on bringing in the Wilko Johnson Band. The reason for this was simple. It was one night back in 1974 that we had slouched off to our local Windsor Castle pub on the Harrow Road to see the Dr Feelgood band of Wilko vintage. Joe came back from the gig absolutely knocked out by the band, but especially by Mr Johnson. He was without doubt one of the main influences on Joe in those early days, as of course Tymon had been when he had actually taught Joe his first guitar chords. Added to this, Wilko had Norman

Watt-Roy in the band, the ex-Blockheads bassist who had also played with Joe in the recording of Sandinista. The other band we got in was built around Vic Goddard ex of Subway Sect, one of the stable-mate bands of the Clash back in '76 / '77, and Derek, my drummer friend from Raincoats and Tesco Bombers days, who had also played with Joe in the mid 80's.

Joe Tribute, Tabernacle, London (2003)
From left: Clive, Richard, Tymon, Jem, Dan, Mick & Tom

The date was fixed for Easter Sunday, and our friend Moira Bogue designed the black and white poster with a photo donated by Jules Yewdall, the ex manager, ex-singer/maraca player of the 101'ers. He also supplied photos he had taken of Joe back between '74 and '76 to Raincoat Gina who assembled a video clip that we were to project during the gig. A sell out was guaranteed by the generous offer of the Rough Trade shop, situated literally fifty yards from the venue, to sell tickets, with all proceeds after expenses earmarked for the soon to be set up Strummerville charity. Mickey organized the sound equipment and technical details with help from ex-Clash roadie Baker, and with this the stage was almost set.

Back in Granada Tom and I went through the 101'ers songs a few times. It really was a tough call for Tom. Not only did he have to take the place of Joe, he had to learn the chords to all the songs, and the words. I booked up a couple of afternoons immediately prior to the gig in a rehearsal studio in North Kensington and we were set to go. The rehearsals went reasonably smoothly, although I must admit there were times when I was reminded of the problems in the 101'ers' band room prior to Joe's abandoning ship. On the second day, Pogues banjo man Jem Finer came down and we went through four or five songs with him.

The gig was unforgettable. For a start there was the fact of being back in the neighbourhood with so many faces from the past, some of which I hadn't seen for almost thirty years. Talk about a walk down memory lane…..and, once the gig started, the poignancy of the occasion. I had more or less thrown open the stage to anyone who cared to say a few words, and whether it was Dick, a childhood friend of Joe, or Jock the Notting Hill Poet, there was nothing maudlin in the air, and it just felt to me as if it was the kind of event Joe would have loved. The main problem was the fact that it was a sell out. The managers of the centre were adamant that no more people could be allowed in, so I had to resort to the normal gamut of ruses to enable the entrance of ticket-less late-comers, many of who were of course old friends who we could not turn away. Apart from the locals, there were fans of Joe from all over Britain and even people who had crossed the pond for the event, so it was with an expectancy in the air that five hundred or so people crammed in to the old hall, bedecked for the occasion with Joe's collection of flags, pulsating now with the sounds from Barry "Scratchy" Myers turntables.

After Vic's opening set and a rather incongruous chat from Jock, Tymon came on with his inimitable music. I joined him on drums for a couple of songs including a version of "Lose this skin" in a style more akin to the "Fools" of twenty five years ago than the Sandinista version that most people might have recognized. Wilko followed with his uncompromising R'n'B, joined on accordion by local man Slim, and finally Esperanza introduced The 101'ers. We rattled through the songs, had Jem come out half way through, and were surprised by the unexpected appearance of Mick Jones - as much a surprise for us as for the audience who went berserk as, with a broad grin on his face, he strummed out the chords of Janie Jones. By the end of the set Derek was also up there on percussion, and finally Simon "Big John" Cassell singing the inevitable finale of "Gloria". By this time the security chief, bouncer, and self-appointed stage manager was having serious problems with the thought of getting home late, but even his threatening and cajoling couldn't prevent a final encore of "White Riot", although he nearly did cause a riot in the dressing room after the gig with his efforts to get us out...

*

Back in Spain, journalist friend Jesus Arias almost immediately came up with the idea of another tribute to Joe, this time in Granada. Must say I was a trifle circumspect with the idea of more tributes and what not. There were propositions involving the reforming of "The 101'ers", which I just couldn't consider without Joe being there, and suddenly various offers to re-release "Elgin Avenue Breakdown". The whole question of jumping on a bandwagon and making the most out of interest in all-things-Joe following his death, is a thorny one. Of course to an extent I am party to that. Nevertheless, the Granada tribute is a case in point. Apart from my personal feelings, it's a fact that there were so many people interested in doing something to remember Joe, and that I, with my contacts and experience in production, was actually in the position of being able to organize it. Joe's birthday in mid August coincided with the date that Federico Garcia Lorca had been shot during the civil war, and through the culture department of the Andalusian regional government I was able to get the promise of funding for the project: a joint tribute to Joe and Lorca. The date also coincided with the fact that Luce and close British friends of Joe would be staying at Cabo de Gata and thus have no problem coming up to Granada for the event.

As with the London tribute I wanted to find a venue with significance in Joe's life. We finally decided on a small open air amphitheatre in the Sacromonte barrio of Granada's old town. Steeped in history and character the neighbourhood has been the gypsy quarter of Granada for centuries, and despite a migration especially in the 60's and 70's to the high rise tenement blocks on the edge of the city, Gitanos still form a high proportion of its inhabitants. It is an area, with its flamenco bars and music, that Joe would have often found himself at six in the morning after a night on the town. The actual venue "Centro de Interpretación" had been recently opened as a kind of ethnological museum dedicated to the traditional way of life of the Sacromonte gypsies, based on the caves in which the majority lived.

The Granada rock band "091" which Joe had produced back in 1986, had since splintered into various other groups and projects, and each of these were keen to play at the event: Jose Ignacio Lapido, Jose Antonio y Quini, Antonio Arias, plus an Italian band "Ratoblanco" who happened to be in Granada, plus long time flamenco character Curro Albayzin who was to recite Lorca poems to guitar accompaniment, and the Clash Dj Scratchy who had come over to spin discs between band change-overs.

As for the "Amigos de Joe" band, the idea was to involve a musician from each of the main musical ventures in which Joe had been involved. Tymon Dogg from "The Mescaleros", Jem Finer "The Pogues", Mick Jones "The Clash" and myself from "The 101'ers", were joined by Tom Lardner's vocals and rhythm acoustic, Derek Goddard on percussion and drums, and Julian Fernández from Spanish band "Siniestro Total" on the bass. It was difficult to synchronize the arrival of everyone for rehearsals, but fortunately Tymon and Julian were able to rehearse for three days with Tom and I before the event as we congregated in Tom's house in a village near Granada. By the time Mick arrived for just one rehearsal the night before the gig, the set list was more or less organized, with Tymon taking vocals on some Mescalero tunes and some of his own; Tom on 101'ers and most Clash songs; and Mick singing a couple of other Clash titles.

Granada in mid-August is a cauldron during the day, and although at night the altitude causes temperatures to drop, the sound check in late afternoon was a sweltering affair, up amongst the bleached white caves and cacti of Sacromonte. My main worry, as in the Notting Hill gig, was the relatively small size for the venue. News of the gig had seared through the internet channels, and the event was sold out a couple of days before hand. With a number of people contacting us and having to be turned away, I started to think we had maybe chosen the wrong venue, but those doubts were dispelled on the night of the concert. The location is certainly unique, tucked in a valley with the Alhambra and the rest of the city spread out below. About five hundred people wound their way up the steep and narrow track leading to it, accompanied by the strains of flamenco guitar and the strident calls of cicadas.

There was a special something in the air that night, that even the dreadful sound quality of the PA couldn't extinguish. Our set was a pretty ramshackle affair as well - inevitably so given the short time we had to prepare it, but a slick performance had never been the intention, and I know Joe would have absolutely loved it if he had been there: it was right up his street. We had a huge vat of sangria back stage at the mouth of the caves that served as dressing rooms and there was a great atmosphere amongst the musicians and punters milling about the place. Our set finished with the incorporation of as many people from the other groups as could fit on the stage, and the party carried on till dawn in a downtown club. For me though, the dual role of player and organizer was a bit much. With so many things to sort out I couldn't really relax and enjoy, which of course was the main point of the event. I'm pretty sure most other people did.

As had happened after the London tribute, there were various calls to establish it as an annual happening. But for me that was enough. I had said goodbye to an old friend in what I thought was the most appropriate way, and it seemed in a strange way to close a circle, to tie-up on itself the thread of an important part of my life that had started back in the basement of 101 Walterton Road, and in which Joe had been such an important instigator. In fact there was just one more project that needed sorting out - a definitive release of

101'ers material. The original "Elgin Avenue Breakdown" vinyl L.P. that we had released on Andalucia Records back in 1981 had long since been deleted. In fact Joe and I had been talking on and off about a re-release for some years: we had even started negotiating with Demon back in the 90's. There had been various bootleg releases on CD and vinyl, including one organized in 1993 without our permission by ex-101'ers roadie "Boogie", but it was Luce who just a few days after the funeral, had mentioned to me that she thought the most appropriate tribute to Joe would be for all his recorded music to be made available.

I started putting the idea to some companies, and with offers from Universal in L.A. and other record labels we eventually accepted a deal with EMI's catalogue division. I had come across more live-gig tapes that Mickey had recorded, including one from a Wandsworth Prison concert and another from a gig in Bracknell just a couple of weeks before the band finished, and then started sorting the sources of all the studio recorded material. EMI were most supportive, and gave me a free hand in track selection and just about every aspect of the project. I went to Abbey Road with Mickey to master the final selection of tunes, and worked with Esperanza on the design of the album booklet with the EMI in-house graphics team. Allan Jones, who had been the first journalist to support the band back in 1975, wrote the liner notes, Jules provided most of the photos, Esperanza supplied some drawings she had done at the time, and I wrote comments for each of the tracks. The album was released in the UK in June 2005 and a month later in the States and most European countries. The object had been to compile the definitive 101'ers album, and for better or worse that is what was achieved. Despite the fact that half the studio tracks were rushed demos knocked off in a couple of hours, and despite the awful recording quality of the live material, taken from Mickey's 25 year old cassette tapes, I think the essence of the band is there. A rough and ready garage band whose forte had most definitely been its live shows, but as the record demonstrates was also capable of putting together a decent song or two. Maybe if Joe had not gone on to stardom in the Clash the group would have been long forgotten, but I'm inclined to think that maybe if Joe had not left in '76 there is little reason to assume "The 101'ers" would not have had the success that many a more ordinary group was to achieve in the changed climate of '77 / '78. Maybe this and maybe that, and quite frankly who knows or who cares…

My memories of those times, the less than two years between '74 and '76, are lodged in a very special space in my mind. Perhaps it is because it was my first band, rather like a first love, or rather like the reminiscences we lucky ones have of a happy childhood, but I have a feeling that perhaps it was precisely because of the lack of "success" of the band that my memories of that time bring such a smile to my face…

Chapter 19   To the present

The evolution of the writing of this Tale has had its twists and turns. My original aim, back in 2001, was to create a "101'ers" web site. This led me to start writing an introduction to the site, which then developed in to the idea of writing the whole story. Having started the project , I mentioned the fact to Joe and we had a long conversation about it. He said he couldn't handle writing anything longer than just the few verses of a song, and besides which his memory was too shot for the task. I don't believe that for a moment!! He could have written a fine Tale, and judging from the reminisces we shared, his memory of those times were at least as keen as mine! His immediate reaction was typical and encouraging:
- "Yea, go for it Snakes...you've got to do it..!!"

I was still with "The 101'ers" period at the time of Joe's sudden death in 2002, and this knocked me of course for some years. When I did come back to it and finished the chapters on "The 101'ers", it seemed only natural to continue the story with Tymon and then the other bands. However, I do get the feeling that when writing of things that occurred 30 years ago, what you lose from your memory banks is more than compensated by the perspective on events and feelings that a lapse of time allows. Conversely, when writing on the present there is very little perspective, so for that reason just a brief summary of present activities seems appropriate...

*

One practical consequence of the Tabernacle and Sacromonte gigs was to be its effect on my work with Tom Lardner. The two of us set about reworking some of his older songs and getting up some new ones, which were to become the basis of a new band: "El Doghouse".   To start with, Tom added a distortion box and cranked up the volume, but retained his electrified acoustic and of course his bluegrass roots. Within a couple of years though, the electric guitar took over completely from the acoustic: at least for live gigs. As for a bass player….. we didn't have to look far. My 13 year-old son Guillermo, (alias Giggs) had been playing drums since he was a nipper, and had recently started guitar lessons. He took to the bass fast and at fourteen was doing regular gigs with us. By fifteen he had recorded tracks in the studio with us for the second album, and apart from innumerable gigs appeared playing on national Spanish TV.

El Doghouse, TVE studios, Madrid, 2005. from lelft .., Tom, Richard & Giggs

More than once I had to come up with a cobbled-together excuse for his missing from a class or two from school, but from the word go he was certain of the direction he wished to take i.e. music. He also played drums and wrote songs for a punk band ("Arseniko") he had formed with his school-mates, which no doubt was a light relief from having to spend time with the Old Codgers, though I'm sure he learned more than a trick or two with us! What an absolute pleasure and privilege for me to spend five years playing music with my son in a working band. Couldn't have asked for more from music!

Within a couple of weeks of his 18th birthday, however, he was on his way to Berlin, on guitar this time with a psychobilly band. He stayed in Berlin a year, enduring a German winter in unheated squats, before moving to Barcelona which is where he is at present. After a year doing piano at a Blues music school he returned to the drums with an exciting offer from Argentinian slide-guitar man Chino Swingslide to join his blues/swing combo "Chino & The Big Bet". He had to get his chops down fast, putting in hours of study, and is now playing regularly in the Barcelona club scene and beyond, with a truly hot band that manages to make a living from its music.

Back in Granada, with Giggs's departure "The Doghouse" was lucky to find a fine replacement bass player in Josu and a tremendous lead guitar player in Eneko. In total the band has a couple of albums, various ep's and a vinyl under its belt, and we are constantly writing new material. Live concerts have decreased in number, but there is one annual event that we never miss that takes place down in Almeria, in the same "Bar Jo" near San Jose, where years back we would so often end up with Strummer in the early hours of the morning. We usually perform on Joe's birthday in mid August. It is an open air venue, tucked away in the desert terrain of Cabo de Gata, but what makes it special are the owner Jo and his team, the music they play there, the crazy metal Jo sculptures that will rear out of the darkness, the customized Harleys, the Strummer-baptized "Toxico" liquid refreshment... We will usually meet up with Lucy there and other old friends of Joe, so it's a great way of celebrating his memory!

I have various other musical projects that come and go, but keep me occupied. In 2011 I teamed up again with Mr Dogg at a studio in Cabo de Gata. We recorded a number of his old tunes from the "Fools" and 101'ers era. Hopefully a release is on its way. Another undertaking has been with Brit Granada resident, Trevor Warren, fantastic composer and guitar player. The music leans nearer to jazz with a lively rhythmic groove, and the participation of various musicians from Granada's jazz scene. In 2013 I reunited with Jim

The Bass in his studio installed temporarily down in the English countryside. The spark was still there between us, and hopefully the project will lead to some finished recordings! Then, back in Granada, there is the Louis Jordan-style blues with Willy James, and hopefully some other yet-to-be-discovered musical idea waiting around the corner... At four in the morning after a gig in some smoky basement-dive with a smattering of punters, cursing, I haul the drum cases from my car back to the rehearsal space in my house, and wonder what the hell am I doing?! But deep down I know. I love it! With luck I'll still be doing it for a good few more years yet.

Luna & Giggs...New Year's eve, 2011

The reception of a brilliantly written travelogue/diary from our daughter, Luna, studying for six months in Colombia, has inspired me, after more than ten years of stop/start, to finally get this job finished. Being a memoir I feel that some kind of summary is in order. From the start my intention had been to write a "Musical Memoir", and one "from the margins" because my involvement in playing music has usually been from the edge of the main stream. Although since my first gig with "The 101'ers" there has been scarcely a time when I haven't had some kind of musical project on the go, there have been few occasions when I have been able to actually made a living from it, and since the mid-80's there has certainly been an ambiguity in my attitude. Despite my love of music not having diminished an iota my difficulty has been to combine the playing of music with finding a way of making it work financially…. to live from it.

If I were to regret any of my past choices, perhaps it would be my failure to have taken up a serious study with teachers of my chosen musical instrument. I was self-taught from the beginning, but maybe should have taken a more serious interest in studying, especially after having rejected the commercial path of pop music. In 1974, when I had first accepted the offer of the vacant drum stool for the 101'ers, it was rather as if I fell in to the world of playing rock music. Perhaps with a greater technical command of my instrument, gained through serious teacher-led study, it might have led to possibilities of playing other kinds of music. Whatever. All pure supposition.

In one respect my approach to music making has been clear from the start: it was so important for me to feel respect for and empathy with my musical colleagues in whichever project I was involved in. If that wasn't present for me in the group….no way could I remain involved. On top of that, a "not suffer fools gladly" attitude makes things difficult when playing in a group situation, and especially when dealing with the business side of music. It is probably true to say that if I had climbed down from my high-horse on more than one occasion, I would have had a much greater success in the field and received the public recognition that a part of us always craves! In the same vein, the scant respect I felt for so much of the Pop/Rock genre, especially its star-system, was to leave me very much out on a limb when I had to make important decisions that would affect my future for working in music.

A burning ambition to be number one I have of course felt, but it was rarely my main motive, and one lesson that we do learn from life is that results are directly proportional to input, and that constancy and force of will are (along with the necessary dose of talent and luck!) the prime ingredients for success. So, given that thirst for success and recognition are the usual materia prima for worldly achievement, it doesn't surprise me that my overall lack of ambition has reaped its measured reward.

As a thirteen year old school kid, I discovered that I was a particularly good distance runner. Suddenly I found myself a district champion, then county record holder for the mile and cross-country. I went to the national school championships and running the mile ended up 7th in the country. All this on an absolute minimum of training and a dubious commitment. I didn't actually enjoy killing myself to win a race and I so much preferred playing almost all other sports especially cricket, my favourite. One day (I was probably 15 years old) the headmaster called me in to his office. I was becoming a bit of a school celebrity, and he attempted to give me a pep-talk and encourage me to train harder and reach for further glories. The conversation stumbled somewhat when he asked me if I enjoyed winning. I considered his question, and replied truthfully that it wasn't that important to me. I told him that there was always going to be someone somewhere better than you anyway, and that I ran against myself rather than the opposition. I'm not sure whether or not he understood what I was trying to say. During my life whether it has been in sport, music or business I have turned down various opportunities for worldly success, and I honestly can't say whether it has been because of my stubborn pig-headedness, my disregard for the opinion of others, or an exaggerated self-importance! Probably a mixture of all!

Life to me seems so much bigger than the dubious rewards of pop star fame. Coincidently, in the late 70's a dear sister of my close knit family was to suffer the pain and sadness of mental illness leading to suicide, and even closer to home we would have to cope with the bipolar mania of my partner. These experiences, both of course worthy of a book to themselves, would put the other sundry events of my life very much in to context. At the end of the day, loyalty, real friendship, and at least an attempt at honesty seem to me the most important values.

Of course all this is relative. I can be seen either as a failed rock muso who didn't make the most of the various opportunities offered; or as a privileged individual who has lived an interesting life full of variety and freedom. I do know that life has given me two exceptional children....one following the musical path of his father, the other the artistic way of her mother. I still share a wonderful life with the 17 year old andalusian gem that I met in a Notting Hill pub nearly forty years ago.

I live in city and country that I adore,

have friends and family of which I could not ask more,

and a drum kit (when not out and about) standing sturdy on my living room floor...

****

Printed in Great Britain
by Amazon.co.uk, Ltd.,
Marston Gate.